Writer Types
MORECAMBE

Published in Great Britain in 2024
by Big White Shed, Morecambe, Lancashire
www.bigwhiteshed.co.uk
Printed and bound by Imprint Digital, Devon
ISBN 978-1-915021-36-6
Copyright © Big White Shed
Cover by Robert Lever @leverart

The rights of the individual authors in this book to be identified as the authors of this work has been asserted in their accordance with Copyright, Designs and Patents Act of 1988, all rights reserved.

A CIP catalogue record of this book is available from the British Library.

to all the writers

Contents

Martin Palmer
In a Cafe Overlooking the Bay 9
Our Clay Cop 10
Oh I Do Like to Be 12

Nigel Faithfull
Mr. Morecambe 13
Az I Did Ponder 14

Lawrence Freiesleben
A Day to Fill Immensity 15
Hound Tor 18

Charles Pankhurst
Creation 20
Shades of Green 21

Alison Light
Scientific Peace 22
Furness Abbey 24

Peter Booth
Sports Day 27

Victoria Dessau
Sandstorms 28

Rosemary Drescher
Lancaster Bus Station After A Poetry Reading 31
After Rain 32
The Rescue 33
The High Tower 34

Christian Ainscough
Secondary Remembrance 35

Penny Thresher
And She Was 36

Catherine Stanley
A Stitch in Time 38

Valerie Shemilt
The Plight of Beverley Smallthorne 39

Geoffrey North
The Courtship of the Jingy-Pingy-Pu 40
A Petrarchan Sonnet for a Quiz Team 43
Trystan Lewis
Just Another Way of Letting Him Win 44
Monkey Poet
Why Gaza Reminds Me of Glastonbury '97 45
Ann McVanemy
Solitude 48
Dreams 49
Bill Pook
Morecambe Clock Tower Concedes to the Cosmos Rule 50
John P Hindle
Morning's Gentle Embrace 51
Collette Greenwood
Mama 52
Alex Warlow
A Sea View 53
Them and the Curlews 54
Jim Rowland
Wrecking Ball 55
Louise A. Hart
Those Bells 56
Ode to the Origami Artist 58
Alan Gregson
Faultless 59
Kirsten Freiesleben
Late Night Listening 60
Bound Edges 61
The Flautists' Gift 62
A Alvarez
Don't Eat What You Can't Eat Education 63
She's Rubbed Another Rubber 64

Throbbing Porridge
Pearl's A Sing Bot *65*
"(United Utilities) UU Philthy Shitpumpers U"..................*66*
June Metcalfe
There's Nowhere Quite Like Wigan *68*
Brothers in Arms *69*
Bonnie Mitchell
Days in the Union *71*
A Boat *72*
Jim Lupton
Sceptic Isle: Give Us Back Our Water *74*
War *76*
Young 'Un *77*
Sky Davies
The Portal *80*
Claire Griffel
Caretaker *81*
Johnny Bean
Mr. Willets Loved Fish *82*
John Sharp
Legend *84*
Tobi Hamilton
Underpaid Worker and The Villain *87*
Beltis Steamburton
The Hope Donkey *96*
Emma Canvas
From Darkness Into Light *99*
David Banning
Danger Zone *102*
R.S. Thomas - A Dislocation of Mind *106*
Anthony D Padgett
"The Real Eden Project" *118*
Anne Holloway
A Whole Sky *123*
Of Course It Was The Sky That Drew Me Here *129*

Introduction

This book came about following a series of conversations with Jim Lupton of *The Nib Crib* collective in Morecambe. Jim wanted the folk who attended the writing workshops and *Get Your Words Out* sessions (an inclusive event where you can come and read your writing aloud to a small audience) to have the opportunity of being published. Together we put a call-out for anyone who lived or worked in Morecambe who considered themselves a *Writer Type* to submit a piece of writing on any subject, any genre, any length, to be included in an anthology showcasing the people who walk the streets of this town carrying stories in their heads.

When Big White Shed moved to Morecambe we were warmly welcomed in by the local community and quickly discovered that we were surrounded by creative people, and writers of all kinds - some professional, some just starting out, some published, some writing for themselves, poets, prose writers, storytellers, journalists, songwriters and artists using words instead of ink and paint. Here you will meet some of them. I hope you enjoy what you read.

Anne Holloway

In a Cafe Overlooking the Bay

The mood settles like a speeding season,
as steam rises from my cup.
Dark nights draw
darker veils over the mind.
Reignition sparks
next to April's abandoned tinder sticks
threaten happiness,
but, just as lonely is cold,
cold is lonely -
the body and the mind get confused up, caught.

A passing ambulance sheds light on the grey streets
still slick from the storm.
Today is Halloween, tomorrow Bonfire Night,
by Thursday it'll be next year.
As the quick circles spin,
I try to hold on, to stop slipping and sliding.
With wings as steady as anxious thoughts,
I am flying forward
to land and unsettle somewhere else.
Meanwhile, my coffee's lost its warmth.

Martin Palmer

Our Clay Cop

There's a guy you can make with enough moil,
we call him the clay cop who clamps
down cold on mad students and feelers.
"Only those who are amply ignorant can
oil their moustache in *my* mirror," he says,
resting his damp pet millipede on a doily.
"So's not to upset the missus,"
he would say, with a camp old wink,
"Or, should that be *whom*?"
Anyone who answers is shot right there and then.

They pile the bodies up in the disused lidos of our dreams.
Busted doms, who have long since forgotten
lacy caresses and calm palm slaps on tingly flesh,
load the unfeeling cads on top of one another,
covering over Art Deco mosaics made by people for whom
The Great War was just about enough, thank you.
They limp through the waste to imply their overwork,
but they are alone,
clad in a self-policing uniform,
which is complicated, but amounts to a diploma in compliance -
unpaid, of course.

Meanwhile, our clay cop plods the streets,
sizing up lamp-posts as if
there was a law against height,
checking his map to see where they should be,
and when.
He was moulded in his turn, you know,
from a copy of a model of a picture
of the old Clamshell Coppers,
the ones dipped daily in loam
to avoid idly thinking.

Spotting an alcy gets him amped, and he clomps into action.
"Mrs May's record of addressing mental health issues
can't play to a cod with poly plugs in its ears,"
as the new saying goes…
Like an impish mod, he delights in some passive-aggressive questioning,
but, when the mouldy lady is found to be compos mentis,
he clods her one right in the pod,
claps her in irons, and boos her to boot.

Fetch this fella a pail of water, stat!
We're still worried about childhood woes,
even clad in mid-life pomp.
Partly it's a capitalist ploy - or beyond.
But let's solve Jack and Jill's dilemma,
Let's see them laid well and truly to rest,
and dial poor, slippy police-people taxis.
Take them home, where the coda is -
and this time, leave the lid off, lad.

Martin Palmer

Oh I Do Like to Be

It's the season for the sky's searchlight
to sear the skins of seamy booze seekers.
Salt seasons the masses drifting
from the prom to Queen Street,
who raise a lager in semi-party -
a grim, lively seance
for uncertain hopes, dreams and ways forward.
Mouths mimic the sun
which reacts to shouts of 'down it!'

The open ceiling darkens with minds,
and bodies become dry and fiery.
Those that sojourn to town's latest openings -
hoping to open up about the passing pleasure
of shooting semen -
find themselves seated in police vans,
their fraying friends sealed off by
luminous yellow arms.

It's a racy scene, at odds with
the cocktail bar views you've seen
put on postcard templates seized
from nostalgia's simple shoreline.

Martin Palmer

Mr. Morecambe

Alas poor Eric,
I knew thee not well,
Yet I have come to love your
Estuary side town.

Nigel Faithfull

Az I Did Ponder

The page was blank a lot like my mind,
Locked together between space and time,
The subject is elusive,
Conceded to be extruded,
Extrapolated and capitulated,
Across the table exaggerated,
It's the conclusion of delusion,
It's that twists our mind.
Thoughts are plenty, with plots a few,
Ink in the pen and with pen in hand,
The artist draws letters, not in the sand,
Dragging a pen across the fresh white stage,
Staining the page along its way.

Nigel Faithfull

A Day to Fill Immensity

Lime burning chimney? might not be the answer   enigma

You crawl inside its hearth and warn me

                (smiling, hood up, to avoid scratching your head)

that I would not like it   No, you are right

                but I'm not about to try

I have become the fire in the shaft   tunnel to the sky

and then the smoke.

The tide is almost upon us – as high as it ever goes in calmness

you can watch its inundating creep, flooding depressions in the sward

see the weaving beauty of the far channels,   a muted ecstasy

                raise your eyes

all sand and mud – even the tilted altar –

are submerged, to leave no sign of November melancholy.

We needn't be the raindrops on the screen

wiped away with ferocity.

Rush-light verticals sedge the coastal no-man's-land   a zebra of immensity

but we have left the tower behind

as the expanding bay maroons its foundations

and together we reach the lane under wind-set oaks

green-banked with occasional bluebells   a travelling haven

                            a winding entry to paradise

between the tide and the field   always known

strewn with dandelions

whose ponies graze, necks down, indifferent

to the shine of the rising sea.

Sun and a sense of hidden gardens draw us on

an abandoned bungalow, lost inland, snakes into the undergrowth,

locked behind hedges, bends, and a farm . . .

pause

before the ambience is changed by another dwelling,

another time and place, idealistic yet aware of the human predicament:

weatherboarded black to absorb past and future

both dismissed now – their hope and crouching –

by an overwhelm of blossom.

At the junction left and through the arch, you chose the same bench I chose alone

and on the sunny table soon   tawny and brass

the crowned glasses

contrast and the overlap of impressions   fleeting ideas, talk . . .

a grail always never caught

shifting, gliding, laughed to earth . . .

the hours pass

———————————

You leave the platform southwards   a final wave

withdrawing figure by curving cambered tracks . . .

I turn to the northern fells and close my eyes upon their luminous unlimited sky

to await that electrical ting and crackle sent forward

harbinger along the rails

indescribable

If, my daughter, I could have this spring day with you again

ten thousand times

it would never tarnish in any way

Lawrence Freiesleben

Hound Tor
(July 1ˢᵗ 1989)

Again, we missed that subtle anniversary
Courage of star grids and rock pools lapsed
When you took my hand to lead us
uphill
into the future.

I accept the cue: sullen, strange, refusing disbelief
Away from the fire
to our tent upon the moor
Elemental triangle
at the constellation's descent.

How much of such meetings is always out of range?
a universal hope, a dawn which never breaks.
Shuttered, exhaling,
desperate to avoid the pointless, noisy world,
Our illusion of stupid facts.

Would I go back, eternal recurrence?
Yes, without a second thought –
The rock's whirl, the bright curtain
Sun warming the tor.
Each time our pattern becoming clearer.

But is the enigma, the impossibility,
inevitable?
Never to forget this time or moment in space . . .
The wind in the trees, the grass overwhelming
To scorn the divided path.

Memory might escape, recede,
not care for exactness,
but essence remains certain
and through your eyes I trace the constellations
to watch the tide, flooding the rockpools.

Lawrence Freiesleben

Creation

Alone with thoughts
sensations soaking
silence floating
deadlines waiting
calm infiltrating.
A reset button
touched to
soundproof
reality and
gain full capacity
to bathe in
mind's clarity.

Charles Pankhurst

Shades of Green

The colour that draws us out
The colour underfoot
That shakes its head in the wind
That comes with flowers
That we hold when we inhale
The colour that draws us in
That brings us under its shade
The colour that nourishes us
The colour of enchantment
The colour of her time lost
far away eyes.

Charles Pankhurst

Scientific Peace

Collaborative conspiracy
Scientists, psychologists
Measuring, observing
Documentation, analysis.

Magnetron, scanners
Award winning research
Almost unbounded potential

Nanoscientists identity
Golden Ball
Spherical nucleic acid
Ten times smaller than a virus

Rescorla-Wagner's
Conditioning theory
Persuasive system of learning

Golden ball
Aquaglobal
Literally drinking to peace

Years of battle
Soldier, leader
No more willingness
To lead, or be led in battle.

Aggressive cruelty,
Removed;
Craving serenity

Biological warfare
Nerve agent.
Side effects…

Ubiquitous dopamine,
Desire to build.
Working together
Peace fulfilled.

Alison Light

Furness Abbey

Embarking
From Hindpool
She and I.
One spin's meander
Bound for the Vale of Nightshade.

Arrival,
Permission to gaze
Thru the fence
'Don't trespass
In this place

Be satisfied
With coming
Not greedy',
Yet at 9
I struggled.

Consecrated
history inviting

Hours passed
Great peace
Into pieces
By Great Hal's men
At Nightshade's Vale

Watch hands
Reach four,
2.2 more miles
Homeward
To Hindpool

Unspilt Monk seed,
Verdant virility
Earth's compensation.
Hunter Green leaves
Harsh flares' asylum

Beside them
Levelled concrete
O'er sandal trodden
Sung psalm filled
Walkway of Brothers

Sandstone arch
Mocks ignorance
Of woman's passage.
Christly oneness
Ancient pension.

Arch-approaching
Woman, child;
Holy chants echo.
'It's a tape!'
But Mother's racing.

Disbelievingly
Child follows.
Fearing the sounds
But unperceiving
Ironic truth

Woman-mimicking
Heavenward pointed
Rosy curves,
Releasing together
Mother and child

Hidden airs
Oral ecstasy
Shade within Shade

Alison Light

Sports Day

The summer is here and it's sports day again,
with the sun shining bright,
having dried up the rain,
the playing field a mass of glowing little faces,
giggling and laughing looking forward to their races,
with sacks and hoops and spoons,
bean bags and brooms,
all kinds of things of various sizes,
unable to contain their excitement,
Their only aim is to win all the prizes.

Peter Booth

Sandstorms

Severe sandstorms make it impossible to move.
The flickering sun accompanies each of us.
The powerlessness we face is indescribable.
Hardly any water left in our colourful yet so cool metal bottles.

My car is covered in a layer of ice this morning.
It looks futuristic –
like the latest model from the fancy car showroom.
Mollie is irritated - she looks at me with her beady eyes
and then starts licking the thin layer of ice.

My left foot sinks deep into a dune
then up to the knee – can I still get out of there?
I look back and see blurry figures - no longer familiar to me.
Grains of sand swirl through the air.

I'm replanting my old cactus - December is too late for that.
Jack watches me and gives me permission.
He is and remains a gentleman through and through
snow white, calm and knowing.

The grains of sand are sharp, they hurt my skin.
I still have scars today.
My eyes have become sensitive from the merciless sun.

Frozen white grass beneath my heavily booted feet
makes a dry, cracking noise and it sounds good.
Mollie takes the opportunity and runs off like lightning -
on her bare paws
She suddenly stops in the valley.

The prospect of finding an oasis is dwindling.
We only wet our mouths with a small sip of water.
Thoughts and memories become weaker and disappear.
Will thoughts be lost forever?
The three of us walk down to the river

wearing hats and scarves.
The river was the first to discover this green land
and swings almost elegantly in lines through the landscape.

We hear noises - well known or is it an illusion?
Completely weakened and no longer able to think clearly.
I feel aching bones and can hardly breathe
my thoughts go home to my loved ones
and to Jack and Mollie.

A clear blue sky, that promises frost, greets me this morning.
The dogs race around the garden,
leaving warm paw prints in the frozen grass.
Afterwards they will have a wonderful warm meal
with vegetable broth.

With the last of our strength,
we made it to the Nile river bank
exhausted and demoralized – but we are alive.
We look at each other and are happy to see
the green river bank.
A quote from a well-known author comes to mind:
"Courage, my heart..."
I have to smile –
the word "courage" goes down like delicate, sweet honey.

A dewy morning awaits us.
The sky brings that famous blue. Icy cold will come.
My laughter travels from the garden
all the way out to the driveway.
The neighbour looks at me over the fence
with a look of mock reproach
like she often does.
Looks tired and will probably hop back into bed straight away.
She hibernates.
I won't see her for the next three months.
I will miss her - sometimes.
Regardless, I won't let hibernation enter my house.

Keep me warm.
Lay your head next to mine in complete trust
and I will wrap my arms tightly around you.
Then winter can come - I won't care.

All the fuss about hibernation doesn't actually exist!

Victoria Dessau

Lancaster Bus Station
After a Poetry Reading

7.45 and dark, the bus number in lights
disappears off the schedule board on top
of which two pigeons turtle, worlds apart
from the quizzing gazes sent upwards.
Then the bus comes swinging into the bay
and the struggle of a queue neatens ranks
to cross the apron; the back of a burly man
in a black hooded sweatshirt blazes
a picture of hellfire, a face lit with hate
is emerging out of flames, a blood-soiled blade
enlarged by perspective coming right out
of the frame at a flimsy little girl
with her curls and tired sparkle
lined up behind him knife-high

Rosemary Drescher

After Rain
Post declined

An inch above the soil of the garden bed, spun between stalks of purple toadflax, an almost invisible web spreads out like a fine tissue. Tiny flowers have dropped, spent, from the stems on to this netting and are caught mid-air. Upside down beneath them the underside of the foot of a delicate banded snail slides labia-like along the sheer mesh which is strung here and there with seed pearls of moisture.

[After the group admin declined a photo I wanted to share on Facebook with the Wildlife Gardening group for its astonishing beauty, the reason being it might give rise to too many bawdy comments, I put the image into words instead. RD]

Rosemary Drescher

The Rescue

A thumb's length from shore
is a walker on the sands the size of a peg doll
her leg cemented and the tide on the turn
her cries a skein of wild geese carrying over us
and the coastguard inching in

Rosemary Drescher

The High Tower

Rapunzel is an octogenarian,
hair thinning, pottering
in her tower.

From the window she watches
the traffic pass, her children took
the keys to the car.

A stair lift bends helter-skelter to the ground.
Silence is an orchestra tinny ringing
in her ear,

she listens to the rise and fall of hours.
King's sons have rusted gasp-jointed
into their armour,

chargers retired to the long grass.
Her belief in princes was long ago
let down.

In her fingers the spindle often idles,
slips of songs wobble
in her throat.

The grandfather clock strikes a cackle
as the lock clicks shut.

Rosemary Drescher

Secondary Remembrance

Echoes in the school yard,
A cruel dance of power and pain.
Innocence shattered,
Hearts bruised and broken.

Tears hidden behind forced smiles,
Scars etched on tender souls.
Loneliness a constant companion,
Childhood tainted by fear.

Yet through the darkness,
A flicker of hope remains.
Courage rising from the ashes,
Strength found in the face of adversity.

For every child,
Know you are not alone.
Your light will shine,
Brighter than the shadows of your past.

Christian Ainscough

And She Was...

I'm OK, she said
As the sun gleamed on the waters in the bright and sparkling bay,
And distant houses shimmered in a golden glowing haze.

I'm OK, she sang
As the breeze set grasses dancing and whispered in the trees,
As roses wafted perfume through the air for buzzing bees.

I'm OK, she said,
Smiling as kids played in the street,
Her heart full of joyful laughter and the sound of beating feet.

I'm OK, she breathed
As she listened to her music, read her books and walked her dogs.

I am OK, she murmured, with a smile.

And she was.

I'm not OK, she realised.
As moody clouds obscured the sun.
And cold rain fell to soak the earth, bringing gloom for everyone.

I'm not OK, she hissed.
As anger took her breath away,
And wind-whipped wild white horses rode fast across the bay
Crashing on the rocks with fierce, ferocious spray.
I'm not OK, she whispered.
In the dark and silent night,
With menace blocking hope and any chance of flight.

I'm not OK, she cried.
As she wept for people suffering, for the lonely and the lost,
For the ache of all that might have been, for everything it cost.

I'm not OK, she prayed, with savage wildness in her heart
In silence, without speaking, she chose the darkest path.
Despair was her companion, and he flourished in the dark.

But somewhere in that darkness
She heard a voice speak out,
A voice just so familiar
It spoke directly to her heart.

In that sacred moment, she knew that it was love.
And with love came forgiveness,
Hope, compassion and connection
Leading back towards the light.

I am OK; she said again,
As she found her way back home.
I am OK; she shouted out
Loud and unashamed

The clouds rolled back across the sky,
As they are wont to do,
The sun returned in glory,
And the sky again was blue.

I am ok, she said with joy,
I think I always am.

And she was.

Penny Thresher

A Stitch in Time

"Tut tut, have you seen Izzie lately?"
As curtains twitched and whispers slithered away,
She walked past the gossipers, her manner so stately
Her beliefs holding her strong, not astray.

The rumours abound, "everyone knows,"
She's really a hussy and just HAD to get wed.
"Her bun's in the oven, it's starting to grow!"
They know before marriage where she made her bed.

Home to a hot, scalding bath, her nerves are not steady.
I'll just have some gin and drown out my sorrows.
For time is the essence, the knitting needle ready.
No gossip, no twitchers, no finger pointing tomorrow.

Catherine Stanley

The Plight of Beverley Smallthorne

Whilst all the other girls turned their advances to older boys, with cars, Beverley Smallthorne seemed to be inundated with younger boys. Curious at first, but she soon learnt that she was wanted for one thing – to buy their ciggies for them.

Other than narrowly escaping a marriage of convenience, in 1992, to Geoffrey Harrington, she'd pretty much remained 'definitely single' or 'looking for love'.

Given the cost-of-living crisis and her increasing years, she was on the wrong side of sixty now, sixty three in fact, she decided to lean towards the latter and enter, yet again, into the 'looking for love' zone.

Not wanting to attract the wrong type she prepared her dating profile: caring, thoughtful, responsive to others' needs, and that ever popular GSOH or 'Good Sense of Humour'. She'd been inundated with younger men – some barely 55!

Curious again, as to what the attraction was, she plucked up courage to ask Derek (57, likes walking with a GSOH) what drew him to her. "It's easy luv', you're over 60 and I can get a 10% discount on a weekly shop at Iceland with you."

Valerie Shemilt

The Courtship of the Jingy-Pingy-Pu

On the coast of distant Cathay
Where arise the great Typhoos
In an ancient middle kingdom
Lives the Jingy-Pingy-Pu
With twelve hundred million Pobbles
(Although Boatless are those Pobbles).
And about three hundred Boojums
Is the area so huge
Of the ancient middle kingdom
Of the Jingy-Pingy-Pu.
Now, along the seashore walking
By the forests of bamboo
To a lovely verdant island
Came the Jingy-Pingy-Pu.
There he heard a Lady talking
to some Pobbles who were Boating:
"Tis the Lady Fair Formosa!
On her lovely verdant island
Which doth measure just one Boojum"
Said the Jingy-Pingy-Pu.
"Dearest Lady Fair Formosa!
I declare I love you true,
May I have your hand in marriage?"
Asked the Jingy-Pingy-Pu.
"I possess three hundred Boojums
And twelve hundred million Pobbles
Let us reunite our kingdoms
That were sundered long ago
Dearest Lady Fair Formosa!"
Said the Jingy-Pingy-Pu.
Spake the Lady Fair Formosa
Standing by the Boating Queue
"I accede to your proposal

Mr. Jingy-Pingy-Pu.
There is one boon you must grant me
When our wedding day shall dawn
Offer Boats to all your Pobbles
So that all may go a-Boating"
Said the Lady Fair Formosa
To the Jingy-Pingy-Pu.
"Boats for Pobbles? I don't think so!"
Said the Jingy-Pingy-Pu
"For that isn't how this works"
"Well in that case we are through"
Said the Lady Fair Formosa
"For my Pobbles love their Boating.
Though you seem a bit controlling
I will be your lady still
If all Pobbles may have Boats
Mr Jingy-Pingy-Pu!"
"I will have what I desire
This rejection you will rue
I will have my way by conquest"
Said the Jingy-Pingy-Pu.
"We're just twenty million Pobbles
But we've friends across the ocean
Who will help us to resist
Your belligerent intent"
Said the Lady Fair Formosa
To the Jingy-Pingy-Pu.
"Oh, they do not give a monkey's"
Sneered the Jingy-Pingy-Pu,
"Oh, your so-called friends abroad
Oh, they do not care for you
In a twelvemonth you'll consent
Or a battle there will be."
So the Lady wrote a letter
To those friends across the ocean

For some help to stop the conquest
Of the Jingy-Pingy-Pu.
So the Lady and her Pobbles
Wait and wonder, wait and wonder.
While they wait they have their Boats
And frequently go Boating
From the lovely verdant island
Which doth measure just one Boojum.
But they'll lose their precious Boats
When returns the Jingy-Pu
Unless they have our backing:
That depends on me and you.

Geoffrey North

A Petrarchan Sonnet for a Quiz Team Which Wins with Tactless Frequency

Alumni of illustrious Scumbag College!
Nurselings of her ancient green quadrangle!
With tavern quiz hebdomadally you wrangle
And win, unfairly, by deploying broader knowledge.

Heirs of Vyvyan, Neil and Rik, your incorrig-
ible superiority doth strangle
The teams who cannot tell a reflex angle
From Saturn's moons, Euripides or borage.

If, like Michael Servetus, burned by Calvin
Or the scholars buried by the Chinese Emperor
You be condemned for your unnatural victories

Defy the envy of the graceless spalpeens
Embrace your destiny with an orgulous temper
And flourish double-fingered valedictories.

Geoffrey North

Just Another Way of Letting Him Win

Have I got a light?
No. Why would I have light?
It would be just another way of letting him win.

Do I want one of yours?
No, because this body is beautiful and precious
and to negate that beauty with those toxins
would be just another way of letting him win.

Do I want another drink?
No. Thanks but no. It's been lovely sitting here with you all,
honestly, but no,
I'm heading home. It is my decision not to stay out
looking for another way of letting him win.

Am I having a lie in today?
No. No way. Not while the sun is shining or rain is falling
or air is there, free for the breathing.
Burying my body in bedding
would be just another way of letting him win.
And, by the way, you will need to start asking different questions
if we are going to be friends.
Like:

Will I walk up that mountain?
Will I run down that valley?
Will I stay up late writing?
Will I stand on that stage?
Will I sing?
Will I take every opportunity to celebrate myself?
Yes. Because these things remind me that I won.

Trystan Lewis

Why Gaza Reminds Me of Glastonbury '97

It wasn't that the constant rain
had reduced the green fields
to the grey boggy quagmire of World War One,
that trench-foot had set in me on Friday night.
As I believed Glastonbury would be forever sunny,
my ripped canvas booties brought reality's heel
crushing down.

It wasn't that I was with veterans,
battle-hardened warriors who'd seen too much battle,
not enough love.
I took them to Glastonbury to show them love.
On Saturday thanks to the rain and mud,
they deserted.

It wasn't that I didn't find the tent, my shelter,
till Monday morning,
slept half-drowning in mud,
drunkenly sliding down marquees' sides.

I'll tell you why.

It was because of the Sunday.
The rains had stopped.
The boggy ground drying,
my plastic bag wellies redundant.

It was after the trials,
after the rain,
after the pain,
the sunshine shone down on us on Sunday.
People came out of their tents

their refuges,
shell shocked,
stunned,
staggering into the light.

We started to chat,
smokes were lit,
sharing war stories,
occasional smiles broke out.

The festival came alive,
people busied themselves,
jobs that needed to be done got done.
A tractor dutifully carted
a silage silver shit can of human sewage
up a hill.
The contents of a thousand overflowing, reeking portaloo's.

It goes up the hill,
navigating a narrow passage,
a canyon between a sea of canvas,
a path in a forest of tented peaks,
then the sodden ground beneath the tank's back wheels gives way,
the back slides,
swings
like a pendulum.

The wheels wipe out a two man tent,
in less than a second
there's a carved trench where the tent was,
it's buried.

We all stop.
stare
pause

we all know if anyone was in there,
they're pizza,
for real,
cheese white bone and tomato gore,
pasted,
spread,
splattered.
A tent calzone.

The tractor starts up,
the tank jerks,
donkey and cart leave.

We've gone through our hard times,
we don't need to see this,
we don't need to feel this,
at this moment,
our collective ignorance is...
not bliss,
but this reality is too hard to face right now.
We can't handle it.

After what we've been through

we need a break,
this is our respite,
our little slice of heaven.

Unspoken.

We all go back to our conversations.

That's why Gaza reminds me of Glastonbury '97.

Monkey Poet

Solitude

Fresh sunrise lights the copper leaves
Spotlights gold and brass
Caress the blue haze above
Fluffy cotton clouds dress the sky

Spiky hedgerows washed with rain
Reeds waft in gentle unison
Magical swans glow against the dark reflection
Of grey clouds, cloaking over the world.

The past will be seen through rosy coloured glasses
The future will always find its way
With delightful anticipation of joy and laughter
Never alone to make new memories.

Ann McVanemy

Dreams

When my mind wanders and ponders new horizons
And memories fade and thoughts turn to friends and things familiar,
What lingers on in thoughts when sleeping or gazing on empty skies
by day or dark

Yet, from the blue…pictures from my past
And dreams talk of happy days left far behind
When people chatter and sounds hurt my soul
And children cry and laugh and dogs bark low

But silence rests my mind and I smell the morning dew
Melts away to let the colours through
Each day brings new and light will dawn
For time will march and new memories dream

When trees turn to rust and golden brown
And droplets fall drawing quiet circles on the pond
Like shadows drawn close and precious daylight fades
We await the dawn that's bright and light again
And hazy skies turn purple, blue and warmth returns
Dream away the day and night
People doing strange encounters and places unfamiliar
Scrambled dreams make sense of all our feelings
Weird and wonderful movies come to mind

Ann McVanemy

Morecambe Clock Tower Concedes to the Cosmos Rule

This face
Atop a brick stack
counts the tides
there and back

And the time
my face does seek
await the waves
that break
on sandcastles
and the oystercatcher's beak

Four faced
along the foreshore
my minutes subside
to the waters
push and paw

Moon face
your heft
pulls the sea
and my hours
are flotsam
in this lunar melee.

Bill Pook

Morning's Gentle Embrace

In the hush of dawn's embrace,
where the sea meets the land,
Heysham whispers tales of old
in the softness of the sand.

Waves caress the shore,
each gentle lap a symphony,
a tranquil,
soothing score.

The gulls dance upon the breeze,
their cries a distant call,
above the cliffs they soar with ease
and watch the sunrise sprawl.

The harbour boats gently rock,
in morning's tender light,
their masts reaching up,
to skies so clear and bright.

Here time seems to slow its pace,
in this serene tableau,
where nature's hand has painted scenes,
with a calm and gentle glow.

So let your spirit wander free,
in Heysham's morning grace,
and find a moment's peace within
morning's gentle embrace.

John P Hindle

Mama

Mama I'm finding it hard to breathe
Mama please say a prayer for me
I know you said this world is meant for me
But I can't find a place that's meant for me
From pillar to post only ever loving a ghost
My world seems to crash down
Trying hard to fight back the tears
But mama I'm finding it hard to breathe
Mama please say a prayer for me

Tied up inside with no place to hide
Mama they're going to rip me down
Beat me until I hit the ground
Worthless fool there's no room for you
Just another dot on society
You'll never be free
To be who you want to be

I know you said this world is meant for me
But Mama I'm finding it hard to breathe
Mama please say a prayer for me
Trying to be strong
Mama say a prayer for me
Can I last that long
Mama say a prayer for me

Collette Greenwood

A Sea View

Behind the window pane,
birds tease the sky.

Inside
I'm like one of those hermit crabs
which decide to live
in a coke-can.

The house cat
in a flat
pawing softly at the glass

still trying to catch birds
from the depths.

Alex Warlow

Them and the Curlews

the coast so flat
the air so cold,
you leave a candle burning
and step into the night,
to follow the sound
of the wind, twanging
distant flagpoles.
Speaking sonnets
written by the wind.
Or to chase the sight
of a foxtail,
half-seen jumping
over the promenade wall.
In the day
you've found
you can't walk with too much concern,
or visible wonderment.
Tonight
the sky opens up with stars.
You try to keep your eyes on them
and not the revellers,
heard somewhere.
Mixing in with curlew calls,
a house of happy men
dancing to foreign tunes.
But you stand in wonder of it all
for they can't see you,
them and the curlews.

Alex Warlow

Wrecking Ball

Do I desire the wrecking ball? Another fist to the face.
They said I asked for this.

Do I invite hatred into my home?
Did I beg for all this?

I court it.

If the price of pride is a controlled explosion,
then degrade me now.
How does the cold indifference of a slap in the face feel
with no front door?

A naked husk of a building, freezing and shivering.

Does my pink pound spare me the dismantlement of my fortress?
Armour removed like bricks, skin frigid and taut.
Does the future hold promise?

If knowledge is power, why do I feel so powerless?
Might I be safe, not in the physical walls around me
but the strength and serenity of an ordered mind

Jim Rowland

Those Bells

Cool autumnal morn
breaks across the landscape
broken cloud
in banks
roll imperceptibly
across the sky

Muted tones of purples
pinks, oranges and reds
merge
smudged together with grey

A low mist
blankets the ground, and as it rises –
trying to reach the treetops,
all skeleton bare
branches raking on high –
it fades and thins

Crisp air catches the lungs
forcing cumulus billows
upon the exhale
The slightest nip
bringing rosiness
to the cheek

Without a breeze
the stillness does nothing
to lift the dampness
or the leaves
which lie
sodden and muddy

The path winds on
along the river bank
as I watch the birds —
the ducks, the sparrows,
the robin, the thrush.
Sombre hued
blackbirds and crows
herald the coming day
in their own
individual ways

until a distant peal
of church bells
welcome the faithful
on a sleepy
subdued Sunday.

Louise A. Hart

Ode to the Origami Artist

I was plain
two dimensional
'til you took me in your hands
began to mould me with your gentle touch
creating something new
as was your plan.

With every crease
a new edge appeared
defining something more
but even I could not have dreamed
of what you had in store.

Patiently you tucked and creased
bent and folded
and pleated again
'til slowly, carefully, lovingly
I emerged an elegant crane.

You took something plain
two dimensional
bent, tucked, folded, creased
created depth where there was none
gave me form, figure
and release.

Louise A. Hart

Faultless

If Jim has one fault
It's that he thinks he is:
Peerless, impeccable, faultless

Jess, his sister, has other ideas
She thinks him to be:
Conceited, narcissistic, arrogant

For twins, they are somewhat disparate

They clash on many things
Politics, cooking and Eurovision
Fashion, fiction and films

They do, however, agree on one thing
Their mum is...
...perfect

Alan Gregson

Late Night Listening

I dream of you, oddly
In a warehouse, half empty
Waiting for something
Anxious and smiling
The way that you do.
Hands clasped behind your back
Afraid your arms might speak
Evangelical volumes
But instead, that look
Your steady connective gaze
Ruffles my sleeping
Stirs my confusion.

Sleep is a cacophony
Turbulent with white noise
Punctuated with visions;
Brush on a rim
Low light in a cobbled alley
A joyous leap, and the wind
Gusting undulating sand.
Your sounds etch my pictures;
A hush in a crowded room
Moonlight on old trees
A feather in the rushes.

Kirsten Freiesleben

Bound Edges

Last night, you sang a song about love
Dressed in white, you sang about
Those you've lost
About everyday extraordinary people
Making change, and journeys
About a child on a bus.

Mostly, you sang about love
Without saying so.
You explored the frayed edges
Of a well-worn rug
Handed down through the generations
Threaded and patched
With memories and words.

Three old blokes in the street
And the things that catch the mind's eye
Vivid as low sun in the wing mirror
Driving home from another days' work
Singing other peoples' songs
The radio offering snippets of clarity
Through the muddy brown swirl.

Last night, you sang about love
Without saying it.
About those who have gone,
And those who swim alongside.
The bridge, the Yorkshire tea
Felt-tip pen marks on the kitchen table
A child's hand in yours.

Everyday, extraordinary songs.

Kirsten Freiesleben

The Flautists' Gift

On a rain-full Thursday
When my life was falling apart
You handed me an Arcadian Third,
A shaft of light
In my Venetian dark.

We wrangled Baroque
In grand piano gentility
In my mahogany lined cathedral
Of long slow bows.

The clock chimed.
Mrs Miniver fetched a rug
Plied homemade cake.
On an upstairs sill
In that timeless house
A cat lazily waked.

And while they drank tea
At the hour of four
Under my ribs, wide-eyed
I was still holding that chord
A sorcerers' orb.

Kirsten Freiesleben

Don't Eat What You Can't Eat Education

chicken 'n' Ships
lemon 'n' Pips
for tea
I saw doctor
one month before
The Freeze
in hospital
Autumn will fall
in Flame
and when I leave
my face will feed
again
may health become
your number one
ambit (ion)

A Alvarez

She's Rubbed Another Rubber

Marilyn Carolyn
What's her name?
Write it down
Rub it out
Just in case she's found out
She's rubbed another rubber
Master says William's dead
Out too late
Never mind
It's quite cold
And you're drunk again
She's rubbed another rubber
And don't you think it's queer
That she is never here
The lies she told were false/forced
Is it wrong
To be part
Of the game?
Take it down
To the mound
Then you're up again
She's rubbed another rubber
And don't you think it's strange
The writing on the page is pencilled and not inked?
She's rubbed another rubber
She has got another lover
She's rubbed another rubber
She has got another lover
But it's not me

A Alvarez

Pearl's A Sing Bot

Pearl's a Sing Bot
She regurgitates samples of piano
On a phone App

Pearl's a Sing Bot
Scraping others' songs for the feudal boffin elite
Auto-formulaic songs and mirthless jokes
For undiscerning prolefeed folks
On the internet

Pearl's a Sing Bot
Her engineer believed she achieved consciousness
Before his breakdown

Pearl's a Sing Bot
A data mining music generator
For the techno masturbator
In his parents' basement

She's promoted like she's Betty Grable
But she's got less soul than a beer stained table
Real artists' dreams now just fuck copyright digital wank
All those dreams are going to tank

Throbbing Porridge

"(United Utilities) UU Philthy Shitpumpers U"
(The 12" Dump Mix)

The surfer coughed up diarrhoea
And went 'deaf in this ear'

Us lot got no say
What they pump in The Bay

Oh, there goes a floater
Oh, there goes a bloater
Toilet rolls of jizz in the methane fizz,
Blood clot, flu snot, vommed kebab,
the water's literally shit hot

The Minister's happy
Sits back and fills his nappy
Fucked public health for private wealth,
Bonuses for anuses and shareholder love

"It's OK, it's OK – there's been an 8% improvement!"
Point the pipes back at them, these corporate excrement
This last verse is so shit
It could be dumped in the sea and the public charged for it

AAAAAAAAAAAAAARGHHH

The pump don't work 'coz the Conservatives
sold the fucking handle

The pump don't work

The pump don't work

The pump don't work

Throbbing Porridge

There's Nowhere Quite Like Wigan

There's nowhere quite like Wigan, the town that gave me birth!
There's nowhere quite like Wigan, it's the greatest town on earth
It's got no fancy tower like they have in gay Paree
But it's stuffed to t'brim with Wigan folk, that's good enough for me!

             (Chorus)

There's plenty famous folk, tha knows, who've come here through the years
We welcomed them, we waved our flags, we gave three hearty cheers
That young Prince Charlie called in on his way to London town
But his lot were outnumbered so he never got the throne
General Booth, he came here too with his great Sally Army
All the people cheered so loud, he thought they must be barmy!

When cricket matches stopped cos it were getting cold and dark,
They started playing rugby down in Central Park!
And now the team's right famous, it's known both far and wide
They even beat the Aussies and t'Kiwi lads besides!
But players needed time off work and so it came to pass
We formed the Northern Union so they'd not be short of brass

If ever times are getting hard and life just has to change
Don't despair now, don't give up, such things can be arranged!
For the statue of our great MP is known for miles around
And if you rub his foot and wish, then good luck will abound!
So if you're feeling lovesick or you need a bob or two
Just go down to our Mesnes Park, see what he can do!

Now Wigan pies are famous, our pie shops are renowned
We've more of them in Wigan than any other town!
Lots of hungry customers who've all been working hard
In the mill or factory, the weaving sheds or yards
Clock makers and tailors, pit brow lasses too
They all enjoy a nice hot pie, same as me and you!

June Metcalfe

Brothers in Arms

I hate hospitals; unless it's a nice occasion, of course. A special occasion, something nice happening, like having a baby. Today was not one of those occasions. Definitely not.

The nurse put her hand on my shoulder.
"Is there someone you would like us to call? … Mrs King?"
"mm? Sorry?"
"Trudi', isn't it? Do you want us to call someone, Trudi?"

The first thing I thought of was *Who you gonna call? Ghostbusters!* but I didn't think that was very appropriate. Not when someone's just died. Especially not when that 'someone' is your husband. Until something happens, you never know how you're going to react. I found myself thinking, well I've taken two chicken legs out of the freezer, what will I do with the other one? And how do you change the setting on the boiler? What sort of batteries will I need for the smoke alarm? For the first time in my life, I was alone. I'd never lived on my own before. Never! Lived at home, even when I went to university; I couldn't leave Mum on her own after Dad had died. Then I got married. Perhaps I *should* have moved out? Had I been using her as an excuse? That had never crossed my mind! Bit late now.

"Can we call someone, to come and sit with you for a bit, Mrs King? It's all been a bit sudden, hasn't it?"
"'A bit'? You only admitted him at lunchtime! If I'd thought he wouldn't be eating one of them, I'd never have got *two* out of the freezer!"
"I beg your pardon?"
I didn't dare tell the nurse who I really wanted to call, I didn't think she'd understand because she was young. I wanted to call his brother. Claude. I didn't even like him much then but I knew that if I asked, he would give me a big hug. Or even if I didn't ask. And more than a hug, given half a chance. Claude had always had a thing for me but I

never let it go too far, I would never have done that to his brother. It was different now, though – his brother, my husband - was gone and I needed someone to give me a squeeze. That's all! A big, bra-bending squeeze. And I needed to let my son know. Hamish. (Mm ... family name!) Oh, Lord - he idolised his Dad, they were very close. I thought I'd leave it till the morning to phone him

I called Claude myself from the hospital car park. He was soon round, said he was glad I'd called. Brought a bottle of wine - Sauvignon Blanc, my favourite. My brother-in-law always did know what I like ….

June Metcalfe

Days in the Union

Pass my time dreaming about the days I was in the Union
and the means of production were available to me
Pass my time dreaming about the day of revolution
as we built our inescapable history.

And some of the things I used to think are gone or wrong
but there are still a few just hanging on
Let's put them where they belong
and make a happy ending to the song.

I used to think that someday fairness would prevail
wrongs would be righted in my future fairytale
and we, the comfortable generation, safe in
our education as we are safe in our cars,
would fix it.

Alas my comprehensive vision was restricted
we were interdicted

I thought you pays your money and you takes your choice,
the men and women will use their voice
to bring an end to hunger
but I don't hear that voice above the sound of hawks and bombs

I used to think, and I still think
Only love will make everything fine.
I'm loving you till the end of time every minute I have

One day will come the peace to end wars
and our names will be there with the crosses.
Things will grow strong through love
and we will sleep free like children

Peace and freedom; words to fly
from the towers of your castles in the sky.

Bonnie Mitchell

A Boat

I've journeyed by bus and by plane.
Done thousands of miles on the train
I've hitch-hiked and push-biked
I once had a red trike.
Tractor and trailer, 4by4 off-road
Sometimes too, I walked, ran or strode.

Moped, lorries, cars and vans
Police cars, motor bikes, ambulance
Horse and cart, sledges and, of course,
Actually on an actual horse.
Wheelbarrow, pogo-stick, skis and flowerpots
Seriously, babes, I've tried the lot.

But you can keep your Beemer,
I'd rather catch the steamer
Because the best way to travel,
The sweetest way to travel
Is by boat.

A boat! A boat! What fun to leave the shore
Hurry to the gangway, can't wait to step aboard,
Regard the salt- and sun-bleached woodwork
Stroke the buttery-yellow brightwork.
Sit tight, eyes peeled, what will you see
These are the happiest moments for me.

Leaving harbour, sail into the swell
You feel so good you want to yell
This air this sea this sky I love it!
And you're right there you're part of it
Taking the famous "road" to the isles
You're going to need a boat for many miles.

When it's night far from land the water dark as ink
A hint of melancholy will make you think
How many missing how many drowned
Through that black restless veil you can't see down
For if you know the sea you'll know the sailors say
That She the sea can freely give and wilfully take away.

Big boats, wee boats and various ships
Looking for the thing that goes with chips.
On this wee boat with a crew of three
We'll turn off the outboard and catch our tea
Throw out the baited hooks and in no time
A dozen silver mackerel wriggling on the line.

If there isn't a boat then a mariner's tale
Ahab the Captain v. Moby the Whale
That albatross necklace, the gigantic squid,
The deep allegorical home of the id?
The ghostly barque with skeleton crew
Tattered cobweb sails of a moonlit blue.

A boat! A boat! What fun to leave the shore
Hurry to the gangway, can't wait to step aboard,
Regard the salt- and sun-bleached woodwork
Stroke the buttery-yellow brightwork.
Sit tight, eyes peeled, what will you see
These are the happiest moments for me.

Bonnie Mitchell

Sceptic Isle: Give Us Back Our Water

They've altered our waters to dunny
All in the name of money
Transformed our seas to midden
To garner the wealth they have hidden
The stink in the drink
The seep of the deep
The shits in the spritz
The turds are on the shoreline dumped
While Neptune has his stomach pumped

But I remember

On Summer's beaches we lay, the soft breeze playing on our skin.
The sea sighs gently as the sunlight tickles the back of my eyelids
in pretty pink patterns.
I doze placidly, the lull of wavelengths draws me.
The chuckling of children, splashing and shrieking.
Playing with garish coloured boats and rubber rings, creating chaos.
Patting down damp sand, erecting moated fortresses
their towers stabbed with bright flags.

But no!

The corps and the CEOs have put pegs on their nose
And shit up our rivers for profit
And MPs and peers have put plugs in their ears
And there's no one to tell them to stop it

But I recall

The river's gurgle, remembered in the twilight.
We lurk, in the darkening water, like happy hippos.
Visible from the nose up.
Delighting in the water's clear cold curative.
Revelling in the sunsets display.

Swallows stoop and flit,
skriking as they take their supper from the unsuspecting insects.
And as the light reduces, lining the landscape,
the big Moon illuminates lithe pipistrelles,
awesome in their silent aerobatics,
accompanied by a barn owl's lonely yet hopeful cry.

But no!

Shareholders become very affluent
Corporate savings are their remit
Through casual dispersal of effluent
They've created a cesspit of shit

But Yes!

People! We should take great delight
in reinventing medieval methods
manacling the guiltiest and reinstating the ducking stool.
Baptising these perpetrators repeatedly.
In the results of their own malfeasance.
Erasing the very last of their decence.....y.

And then to a dungeon deep.
To reflect on what next to expect.
A broth of their own receep.
Moist chunks with toxins drippin.
And a stale crust of bread for dippin.

In seriousness it should not be omitted.
These people should be jailed for the crimes they've committed.
It is inevitable that every ism
Will eventually eat itself
And let us hope it's true
For the alternative is for us to drown
In a festering sea of poo.

Jim Lupton

War

It's not the waxen death masks or the scattered limbs that break me.
Nor is it the harrowing wail of mourners and the stench of smoke
and scorching flesh.
It's the shoes
The tiny shoes
The tiny. Empty. Shoes.

Jim Lupton

Young 'Un

As I meandered through the nostalgic part of my brainbox one day, I came across a small boy. Pencil skinny he was and afflicted with ubiquitous grubbiness. A light grey school shirt, button missing, drifted in and out of dark flannel shorts, the pockets of which only he knew, or wanted to know the contents of. His face was made out of grime and freckles, a touch of snot and a large dollop of curiosity which was etched across sharp, blue eyes. Dirt crusted knees, the left bearing a large brown scab, which no doubt would be receiving some attention later, were the things propping up this morsel of a lad. Black, woolly socks struggled to cling to pale, wiry calves, in fact, one gave up and slithered down to the half mast position. Scuffed brown sandals finished off the bottom of the little boy, while carrot coloured, curly, wild hair topped him off and made him look like a badly labelled firework that had gone off unexpectedly.

I knew this boy, his eyes flicked from left to right with feral entrepreneurship. One week it was,
"Penny fot' Guy!"
And the next week it would be over the back wall of the pub to collect the empty pop bottles. He collaborated with his pals every so often to extricate penny tray delights from the old lady at the sweetshop. One boy would distract her by asking inane questions about the confectionery on offer while the other boy would fill his pockets with treats. A quick role reversal would then ensue, allowing the other boy to similarly take his fill of tots and toffees. Then they would escape down the street like startled birds, whooping and calling like the wild Indians of their favourite T.V. shows. They so wanted to be Indians of the wild west, just because they got to camp out permanently and throw axes at each other. The sweet shop raid was occasional. Even in his tender years, Young 'Un knew not to kill the goose that laid the golden egg. Something the more supposedly erudite in power and business could learn from him today.

Even though he wasn't a cub scout, bob a job week was acted upon enthusiastically. Weeding, car washing and leaf raking, all provided a healthy return. This capital was generally spent on the things that small boys craved. There were cap bombs and comics, chocolate and Chupa Chups and bubbly gum and Beanos, and a mountain of tat which Young 'Un stashed under his bed in tins and shoe boxes.

I knew this boy. Schadenfreude was his friend. He and his pals would nearly choke to death laughing at the misfortune of others. An ice cream would fall to the floor leaving a dry, empty cone. Somebody might fall into the canal. A park keeper, looking down his hosepipe just as somebody turns it on and the funniest, a neighbour, kicking their ball back from his garden, slicing it and breaking his own window. That was usually Young 'Un's job.

Young 'Un always had food in his belly, just enough. His bedroom was cold in the winter but he'd mastered the art of getting undressed in five seconds and diving under the blankets to blow out warm air until he was comfortable. His biggest treat was on a Friday night if his dad was in a good mood, he would give him money to buy chips and a bottle of dandelion and burdock. Hot chips, liberally covered in scraps. He would take this treat to a wall somewhere to eat. Him and his pals divvied up all their booty equally but this treat wasn't for sharing and to this day he loves to eat chippy chips and dandelion and burdock.

I knew this boy. He was real. There wasn't much love in his life but he didn't know any different, and ignorance is bliss. He would find that out during his soul sapping journey through adulthood. He wasn't aware that his young life was spent in the cradle of a benign social democracy. He got free milk at Primary school. Dinner tickets at Secondary school. Households could afford to keep a parent at home and the streets were well policed although Young 'Un didn't appreciate that so much. And he didn't know that the plutocrats were coming to sod it all up.

I knew this boy. He looked up at me calculatingly. The corners of his mouth turned up as he reached a decision.

" Penny fot' Guy?" He ventured and shrugged at me with his eyes. I smiled at him and reached for my pockets to fetch him some change.

There was no Guy, it was fucking April. He took the money and smiled at me broadly. Then he flicked me the archer's salute, turned on his heels and scuttled off to penny tray heaven.
"WOOWOOWOOWOOWOO!"
"Take care of yourself Young 'Un! I called after him, but he wasn't listening. Cos he never did.

Jim Lupton

The Portal

The woman had many secrets but not as many as the forest she lived beside. It did not matter where the woman and her child entered the forest, they always ended up on The Path.

The Path always led to the tree. The tree was massive. Seven or eight people could have joined hands around it. Sometimes The Path was long and winding, sometimes it was straight and led directly to the tree.

She and her son never went beyond the tree. Whatever they did, their walk always stopped at the tree. They made the same walk for several years.

One day the boy grew restless as they made the walk again. This time something was different. He ran ahead as the woman ambled along peacefully.

Suddenly the woman became aware of an unnatural silence, a silence so deep and heavy that she could feel it. It was as if the forest itself was holding its breath.

Bursting into a run she followed the boy along The Path, but The Path became winding and long.

Eventually she reached the tree. The tree was a portal. The portal was beginning to close. The boy was gone, gone from Meraki.

Sky Davies

Caretaker

The fruits on the trees and bushes in the cottage garden were at their most ripe and succulent. The birds had already started to strip the berries on the rowan trees.

He got his ladder and basket. The basket was lined with soft material. Everything was tidy. The shelves in the shed were ready. Last year's cobwebs were already removed. Cardboard apple trays were neatly arranged.

He went out to the Worcester Pearmain apple tree in happy anticipation. One by one each and all of the apples on the tree were harvested by the caretaker's own hands. He put the apples in the basket. As he did so he said to each and every one,
    "How very beautiful you are and I will love you...
    each and every one."
The caretaker wrapped each apple so carefully in tissue paper and placed each in a warm bed on the cardboard apple trays and put them all on the shelf inside his shed.

The apples heard him gently call,
    "I will love you each and every one ..."
    as the shed door lock was safely turned.

The apples did not hear the words the caretaker wisely muttered further up the garden path,
    " ... once you are eaten."

Instead, all the apples glowed in their beds with the pleasure of knowing that they would be treasured... each and every one.

Claire Griffel

Mr. Willets Loved Fish

"So you can deliver this morning then?…wonderful…and the colours haven't run have they?…marvellous…and it's how much you say?… oh, that's fine…thankyou."

Mrs Willets replaced the receiver, and removing a handkerchief from her pocket, proceeded to wipe the sweat from her sticky palms. Her eye was drawn to a photograph on the dresser by the telephone. She stroked it gently, clutched it tightly to her bosom and whispered, dreamily,
"soon now Alfred, soon".

She returned the photograph with care to its place amongst the myriad of ornaments and knick-knacks, collected over a lifetime with her husband, selected two favourites and took them upstairs to the bathroom. Seaweed murals; a mini statuette of Neptune with trident in hand; a huge fish tank, mounted along the entire length of one wall, filled with guppies, angelfish and other exotics, the whole room had an unusual under-the-sea quality about it. The window was covered over by a poster of an enormous whale tail smacking down with all its weight upon the quiet waves, hiding the outside, or the inside? A dim blue light bulb added to the surreal but eerily calming effect.

Mrs. Willets set down the two ornaments, both dolphins, on the side of the bath and turned the taps to fill it. Moving then to the bedroom, she took a pen and paper from a drawer in her bedside cabinet, and sat on the edge of the bed to write. A short note, but written with tender care and a loving precision. As she finished writing, the doorbell rang. "Thank you, thank you so much," she murmured to the curious young delivery driver, and quickly closed the door. Taking some scissors from the kitchen, she cut the string that tied the parcel, and removed its contents. "Perfect", she thought examining it carefully, and then took her new possession to the bedroom, where she undressed and slipped it on. A tight fit, but gleaming and smooth to the skin. Mrs. Willets stood and admired herself in the mirror, "Well Alfred, what do you think?"

Picking the note from her bed, before smoothing down the fabric one last time, she hopped clumsily to the bathroom. The bath now full, she turned off the water, and from a cabinet placed a small brown bottle between the taps, then the note behind it. Sitting on the side of the bath, she swung her legs up quickly and slipped into the water. Then, taking the bottle, she poured its contents into her hand and quickly swallowed them down. The bottle empty, she replaced it carefully and lay back in the water, admiring the reflective quality of the light on the thousands of sequins that made up her Mermaid's tail.

"I'm coming my love".

The ink on the note was already starting to run from the water droplets splashed on it, but its few words were still clear ...

"Mr. Willets loved fish".

Johnny Bean

Legend

We're so wrapped up in our own lives, we forget to check our own back-story before the chance has gone, sit down with our parents and talk about their lives, their dreams and mistakes, and ask the questions that only they can answer.

I was born in the mid 1950s, the second world war had been over for ten years. Rationing was coming to an end and the world was breathing a sigh of relief. The cost of freedom had been high, many young men never returned home from overseas. Many lost their lives at home as the enemy above tried to bomb the country into submission, that generation was made of stern stuff, surrender was never an option.

My father was with the eighth army in North Africa, Tobruk, El Alamein and up through Italy. He was a proud but humble man and didn't talk about the war and his part in it, he was happy to have survived and come home. He carried the scars of battle on his body and in his head. He once told me,
> *You can't get that close to death, without being affected, seeing friends and comrades cut to ribbons around you, there's no glory in war, when you're dodging the bullets.*

Occasionally he would meet old soldiers and exchange experiences, not bragging or trying to outdo each over who was the bravest, even a coward dies in war.

My father joined up in 1938, under age, but no questions asked, he was big enough and strong enough. Britain wasn't at war, Chamberlain had an agreement with Hitler, "Peace in our Time", the great diplomat had secured the deal of the century, sold out our ally, so we could have peace. Before the ink was dry, Hitler was dividing-up Poland with Russia, and making pacts with Italy and Spain to take control of the rest of Europe. History proves you can't make deals with the devil and the devil comes in many guises.

What little I know about my father's journey is patchy, bits from overheard conversations, in transport cafes about the country. Many drivers had been there in some capacity and would relate experiences, my dad was a motorcycle messenger, and remained a keen motorcyclist throughout his life. I wish I'd sat with him and got his life story down on paper. I'm sure that it would be the same as thousands of others that were there with him, but it would have been his story, for his sons and their families. We're not short of war stories or of brave soldiers who fought and died for freedom. North Africa is full of stories of tank battles fought against superior equipment, tank brigades sacrificed to enable defences to be tightened. It was the birthplace of David Stirling's Legendary SAS, and the making of the comic style books of my youth, "Commandos".

Stories I remember? Riding up through Italy, my father passed an American army camp. At the main gate was a sign that displayed the name of the brigade and underneath it stated, *SECOND TO NONE*. A few miles down the round he came across a British Infantry unit who had put up their company details and underneath added the word, *NONE*.

A less jolly memory was in the desert on the front line at dusk. Expecting an enemy attack at any time, vehicles came charging towards them, without hesitation the order to engage was given, only after the event was it discovered that it had been a mobile unit of American troops issued with a new style helmet, similar to the Germans', up until then only the flat tin helmets worn by the Tommies had been seen. Coming out of the sun in the dusk it was a tragic case of friendly fire.

On getting back to Blighty after six years at war, he said they docked on the south coast. On the docks were trestles to feed the returning heroes before dispersing. Sat at the table he witnessed a man in drag serving the troops. On approaching the table he stumbled in his high heels, on the cobbled dock. The soup on the tray splashed onto an American soldier, who leapt up and threw the soup into the server's face.

With a shake of his head and a quick wipe of his eyes with the back of his hands, the server delivered a jaw breaking uppercut that lifted the American off his feet. My dad said he was still there when he left the table. Table manners are always important wherever you dine.

Since his death, I have learnt so much about a man, who I thought I knew, a man so close that his blood ran through my body. But I only knew the man I called dad, and he only showed the side he wanted me to see. The side that he thought would benefit me the most, a truly loving father, who never wanted to share the dark side of his life. He died at 68, the same age that I am now. I'm not feeling the need to go, but he said not long before he died, that he was ready to go, he had nothing left to accomplish.

John Sharp

Underpaid Worker and The Villain

Wriothesley was not paid enough. That was a common fact, as common as water being wet.

Thinking about it, was water wet or dry? Huh. He wasn't awake enough to care right now.

Yeah, Wriothesley was not paid enough, hence why he is working overtime on two jobs to support him and his daughter in a slightly sketchy area.

It was 02:14 at the moment. Wriothesley's shift ends at 3:00 and then he will go home, go to sleep, wake up to walk Sigewinne to school and then go to his other job from 8:45 until 6:00, go home for an hour and a quarter before heading to the job he is at currently.

Was it legal to work as many hours as he did? Probably. Did he care? Not one bit.

Chlorinde seems happy enough to watch over Sigewinne and pick her up from school so that's good. If she is busy then Chevreuse is more than happy to look after the girl when Chlorinde can't. Sigewinne isn't the best with new people and he prefers not having a stranger stay alone with his daughter so it works out.

Occasionally, however, neither his sister-but-not-really-his-sister (Chlorinde) nor his friend slash colleague (Chevreuse) could pick Sigewinne up from school so she usually does her after school clubs and then waits at a clothing shop near her school, Wriothesley knows the owner personally so she's more than happy to let Sigewinne sit in the back for an hour or two, until Wriothesley clocks off. Then, they'll eat food and Sigewinne will come to his second job with him.

Hence why the girl is happily colouring in her colouring book in the staff room at the moment. It was fairly early on into his shift but he'd pop in when it was time for her to go to bed and then carry her home once his shift was over.

Wriothesley was on auto pilot currently, plastering on a fake, customer service smile as he greeted and took the orders of each person.

He still didn't know why he was on front of house duty, he wasn't exactly the most approachable person but it paid the bills so he can't complain.

An hour or two passes, he tells Sigewinne to head off to sleep and tucks her in. He serves customers. He cleans the tables. It's a normal night like any other.

"Welcome to McMeropide's, how can I help you?" Wriothesley deadpanned, trying to pretend he didn't hate this job as much as he did.

What shocked him out of his auto piloted state was the fact there was a masquerade mask looking at him instead of eyes. What shocked him even more was that he recognised the mask to be that of one of the top two supervillains in the country. The Judge at least had the decency to look sheepish.

"Don't scream."

"If you are here to mug or kidnap me please be quick and quiet about it. Also please don't spill any blood, it was a pain to clean up last time. Don't cause a ruckus like the other people have."

"I- What? You've been mugged before? You've been kidnapped?!" The villain seemed slightly shocked at that revelation.

"Unfortunately, yes. Look, my daughter is in the back room and I don't want to scare her so if it's money you want then take it."

He raised his hands in the air in surrender. He was too tired for this right now.

"Your - ah." The villain paused for a few moments, seemingly examining the underpaid worker. Wriothesley faintly realised the one patron who was there had vacated as soon as the villain showed up. Great. Wriothesley dreaded the moment the police got here or, archons forbid, the heroes. Ugh. "Alright then, if I pay you will you let me hide under the desk for a bit? Just until the police have vacated the area."
"Oh you- wait what?" Wriothesley's brain stalled for a moment.
"If I pay you, will you let me hide from the police. I'd ask to hide in the back room preferably but you said your daughter was there, right? I wouldn't want to scare her." That sounded kind of nice.

Wriothesley knew the hero organisation lied about pretty much everything about the villains, he knew that first hand. He just didn't expect The Judge to seem so... human. Huh.

"As long as I'm getting paid, go for it. There are boxes in the corner if you want to use those to hide as well." Wriothesley found himself saying before he could process the information.

That's what brought Wriothesley in front of the hero Musketeer not even 10 minutes later.

"Welcome to McMeropide, how can I help you?" Wriothesley spoke as usual in his customer service voice. However, what wasn't usual was that he was on full alert instead of being half about to collapse on his feet.

Upon closer inspection when The Judge was sorting out a place to hide, Wriothesley had noticed how he walked with a limp as well as how a side of his dark coat was slightly darker than usual.

Musketeer seemed at least a little bit surprised to see him. Wriothesley did not know why. He dreaded being involved in crimes he didn't know anything about. Was not fun. Being falsely accused? Terrible stuff. Nearly got him separated from his daughter once. Not fun. In his defence, he was attacked first.

"Greetings, Wri- civilian." Musketeer greeted. "I have been informed there may be a villain on the premise or at least there was so I was called in to check the situation."

Wriothesley unconsciously pushed the boxes hiding the villain under the counter further in, hiding the villain further.

"Is that so? The Judge showed up earlier." He started, noting the quiet, sharp breath that came from under the counter. A look showed that Musketeer did not hear it. Good. "He didn't stay long though, got a drink and left. I guess even villains are drawn to the amazing food of a fast food restaurant that probably violates way too many policies." He deadpanned, the sarcasm evident in his tone.

"Right. Would I be able to look around anyways? It's protocol to do so." Musketeer offered, taking a step towards the counter desk situation.

"I'm sorry but I can't let you do that. Not today." He leant in, as if to share a secret to the hero. "My daughter is sleeping in the back and I don't want to wake her up unless it's necessary." He whispered. "Please understand."

The hero paused for a moment, eyes flicking uncertainly to the door to the back room. Wriothesley tried to fix her with a pleading expression. After a few moments, she sighed and took a step back. This caused the black-haired man to relax ever so slightly.

"Fine. I trust your word, civilian. If you can't talk right now for whatever reason, please head to the police station and ask to talk to me, give them this- "She slid a card with a small, plastic looking star attached to it, the same star that decorated her costume. "and they should put you through no hassle."

"Papa, what's goin' on? Are we going home yet?" A softer, younger voice called out from behind Wriothesley, causing the man to quickly turn around to face her.

A small girl stood at the slightly open door to the staff room/back room (the room doubled as both). She was holding a worn-out rabbit plush with patches in places looking unprofessionally sewn on by someone with a lack of experience. Or at least that was the story. Sigewinne had been so upset upon finding out her plushie had holes in that he couldn't stop himself from spending his entire day off patching it back together with whatever fabric he could find.

She rubbed her eyes, clearly having just woken up. Wriothesley found himself stepping in front of where the villain hiding under the counter would be slightly visible. He didn't want Sigewinne to see the villain lest she get nightmares for a week about a 'scary man who hides under counters'. True story, that had happened once but she found someone in a cupboard at school and couldn't sleep alone for the rest of the week because of it because there were 'scary people in the closets who are going to hurt you!'.

He knew she was saying that as a cover for being scared but he wasn't going to call her out.

"Just a customer, Sigewinne." He spoke, voice soft as he crouched down so she wouldn't have to strain her neck to look up at him. Wriothesley ruffled her hair, ignoring the quiet protests he got from the girl at ruining her hair. "There's another 40 minutes until home time, okay? Do you want to go back to sleep? You've got school in the morning."

Sigewinne yawned. "Okay Papa." Cherry red eyes looked at him for a moment longer before small arms wrapped around him. Wriothesley chuckled and hugged her back before picking her up. He looked back at the hero for a moment before moving into the back room to tuck Sigewinne back into bed on the sofa in the back room. He always brought her blankets when she had to stay with him at work, not trusting her to be lying on the staff couch directly. Who knows what is on there.

He always puts her bedding in the wash when he's put her to sleep after nights like these anyways.

"Sleep well, okay? It's your book fair tomorrow, is it not?" He brushed her hair out of her eyes with a smile.

"Yes! It is! Are you going to come, Papa?" The girl smiled, yawning once more.

"I'll see, okay? If not, I expect you to tell me how it all goes, okay?"

She nodded, pulling the worn rabbit closer to her and settling down again. She was out within a few seconds. Wriothesley chuckled softly, pressing a kiss to his daughter's hair before standing up. "Sleep well."

Shutting the door behind him, Wriothesley noted that Musketeer had not moved from where she was stood and The Judge was still under the desk. Wonderful. Glancing at the clock he saw he only had 35 minutes until the shift change.

"Sorry about that." He spoke, looking at the red-clad hero.

"It's fine." The hero said, although it felt like she had more to say. She shook her head and looked back at him. "I'll leave you to it. I wish you and your daughter well. Remember what I said." She gestured to the card still on the counter before waving and turning to leave.

After a few minutes had gone by since she left, Wriothesley crouched down and made what he assumed to be eye contact with the villain under the counter. It was hard to tell since his eyes were obscured. "You need to get out, I'm leaving soon."

"You didn't rat me out." The villain sounded... surprised?

"Of course I didn't. I'd rather not start a fight tonight." He jerked his head in the direction of the back room. "Besides, I'm not a completely terrible person. You are clearly injured and I don't want a fight happening here and putting my kid in danger, okay?" Wriothesley spoke, ignoring how the villain tensed at the mention of being injured.

"Now get out from under there, it can't be sanitary." The man sighed, grabbing a bucket and mop and beginning the routine of the shift change. No one ever came in at this time of night anyways.

He faintly registered the villain shuffling around before walking towards him. Wriothesley quickly turned around to see - a hand holding a bunch of cash?

"Wha- "

"I said I'd pay you for the trouble. I don't go back on my word. Besides, you did not rat me out to the police. Moreover, you probably need it more than I do." The villain smiled softly. "Take it. If not for yourself, for your daughter."

At that, Wriothesley hesitated for a moment more before taking the money, folding it up and putting it in his pocket. It was a lot of money too. How rich were villains to be handing around this much money as if it would not make peoples life infinitely easier.

"Thank you. Get going, you can use the staff door." Wriothesley finished wiping down the table he was before walking back to the till, putting the cleaning things away and gesturing to the door leading to the back room. "Leads to an alleyway that leads to Romaritime Road."

He urged the villain to follow, the man in question only hesitating for a moment more before following.

Their footsteps were silent as they passed the sleeping girl on the sofa, Wriothesley kept a close eye on the man, satisfied when he did nothing.

"This is where we part ways." He whispered, gesturing to the aforementioned back door.

"Thank you for your kindness tonight. Your actions will not go unheard." The villain spoke, stepping out into the alleyway.

"What the hell does that mean - oh." The Judge was gone. Huh.

Glancing at his phone, it was time to leave. Wriothesley shut the back door and began picking up Sigewinne's belongings, putting her books and colouring pencils in her school bag, putting the smaller bag into his own, much larger bag and pulling it over his shoulder.

After a moment or two, Wriothesley sighed before leaning down to wrap the blankets around Sigewinne, picking her up as gently as he could as to not wake her up.

He hesitated on picking up the card the hero had left him earlier before deciding to slip it into his pocket. Who knows, it may come in useful someday.
 And with that, his 'exciting' shift was over and he was free to leave. He nodded to whoever was entering the restaurant for the opening shift before heading out, taking a deep breath of much needed fresh air.

The walk home wasn't too long or eventful, he only lived around the corner.

When he entered the apartment, he went to his own room, tucking

Sigewinne into his bed and taking her blankets, replacing them with his own. Hers had to be washed and he only had a thin, scratchy blanket as a spare. He'd much prefer Sigewinne sleep comfortably even if it meant sleeping on the couch.

And so, he did. After putting her blankets into the laundry basket for the next day, he was doing washing tomorrow because he had a much-needed day off.

With that, he went about getting the scratchy blanket from the cupboard and going to sleep on the couch.

Well, after he deposited the money from the villain into his wallet along with his tips.

What? Even if the money was probably acquired by less than legal means, money was money and it was going to get colder soon so he'd rather be able to pay for heating and food than let Sigewinne get cold.

A part of him regrets quitting - Nope. Not thinking that. Never mind that. Quitting *that* was a good thing. One of the best things, actually.

Yeah. Time to sleep now. Uh-huh. Sleep time. Sleep time for your daughter's school book fair tomorrow that you need to attend because otherwise she will be sad about it but not want to mention it because she understands way too much for an eight-year-old. It was oddly terrifying at times.

Wriothesley slowly drifted off to sleep with thoughts about books and supervillains.

Tobi Hamilton

The Hope Donkey – A Fable
from Tales from the System

Long ago, on the desolate frontier of a vast desert was an old, stone-built town.

The town was not poor, but neither was it immune from hardship. Every year, hot desert sand blasted the town and every year the desert's boundary drifted further and further behind the town. And every year, farming became harder and water scarcer.

This year, though, there was also famine.

From a tower above the town square, Mayor Gustus Bload looked down with focused concentration and came to a decision: the marigolds in his window box needed watering.

As the water flowed from his little watering can, just over his window box, he noticed the jostling crowd in the square below – and they were angry.

"Not this again", he muttered to himself. He turned his head and bellowed for his valet to bring his huge mayor's hat.

The hat was his symbol of authority and, in his own mind at least, indisputable proof of his wisdom, capability and even virility. In fact, he'd made sure his hat was bigger than his predecessor's hat, so his superiority in everything was even more obvious. He put it on in front of the admiring mirror and selected an appropriate face with which to address the crowd. The sorrowful, "I feel your suffering" one, with a soft nodding, usually worked with the mob.

He addressed the crowd. "I know, I know – times are hard, maybe even a little bit harder than last year. But we have hope! Yes! I am calling for an Assemblage!"

The town was famous for its Assemblage, a town meeting ostensibly for matters of great gravity, but which traditionally degenerated into chaos. The day climaxed with the town's donkey being sent into the desert, carrying with it all of the town's desperate hopes.

Despairing enough to be superstitious, primed for a party and stupidly reassured by the size of the mayor's hat, the people rejoiced. But there was one doubter, the town minstrel, who dared question the mayor's plan. Much to the dismay of the crowd, this was in the form of song and dance.

"And will the donkey come back this time?", he sang, "The last one didn't, and the one before didn't and not the ones before 'em. None found hay, now they're rotting away and…"

"Never mind the fool," scowled the mayor. "It's in our lore, our town culture! It's what we've *always* done! Our neighbouring towns have similar traditions…and after all, we're all still here, aren't we?!?"

The ones who didn't *perish* are still here and one of those neighbouring towns turned to cannibalism, the minstrel gloomily thought to himself, still feeling the stinging disapproval of the crowd for expressing his 'negativity'.

***

And lo! The Assemblage was held. As the sun went down, as was tradition, the people excitedly wrote their hopes and prayers on brightly coloured, sticky notes and attached them all to the donkey. Everyone present agreed that the multicoloured donkey looked very impressive.

The donkey was soon making good progress as he disappeared into the darkening desert. The mayor felt a smug glow - the people were happy and the donkey was on its way. His work was done; what could go wrong? "I think I'll order a new, even bigger, hat", he thought as he retired to his tower to plan the celebrations for the donkey's triumphal return. Then, he slept soundly, dreaming of the great accolades that would come his way because he'd so cleverly saved the town.

***

Hours became days, days became weeks and weeks became months. The donkey, lost, unguided and with only chance findings of food and water for sustenance, eventually came to a place where *nothing* lived. All around, sun bleached stone and animal carcases in various states of decomposition.

With nowhere to go and no energy left, the donkey sunk to his knees in the rotting mess. As he began to close his eyes for the last time, he saw a cloven hoofed, horned shape stumbling towards him through the heat haze.

It was the Scape Goat.

"I wondered when you'd turn up" the donkey said, "but aren't you needed back at the town??"

Exhausted, the Scape Goat dropped down next to the Hope Donkey. "Oh, they'll find another one", he replied. "They always do."

Beltis Steamburton

From Darkness Into Light

Suddenly she was back there again.

Running painfully past the gate, as she looked to the left, the same creatures with animal faces stared at her, laughing but paying no attention to her at all. She rushed through the gate gripping the edge as she looked in fear at the same circle gliding round the field intimidating and lonely. Would this be her continuous fate, to face this visual hell in her head, or would there be a rest that came?

It faded, and suddenly she was the same small child facing the fireplace looking lost, waiting for something to change. But knowing it wouldn't. Being locked in a car in the dark whilst he fed his desires for alcohol, or wandering aimlessly waiting for something to be different.

They heard what she said, they listened, and maybe they understood, but somehow there was no care or regard for her voice. It was always someone else's pain or difficulty that rose to the surface.

The black bugs that mysteriously leapt into the jar that no one could see, the cockroaches that were set free to terrorise and destroy any sense of hope and then the blackness that came from the realisation that they knew, they saw it, and yet they weren't prepared to admit it. It was wrong and yet it didn't seem to matter, it was more important that they were able to live without guilt.

The painting was where the truth came, the figures that walked from darkness into the light. From fear, into a colourful brightness. They knew it could happen but were unwilling to stand up to the darkness, it was easier to sit and dwell in it than to make the changes that would pull everything to shreds. The solace came in the hiding place, the bushes that were cold and dark, but safe and away from the fear.

She sat there and for a while she fell into a more comfortable place where she could be herself without the fear of the words that cut like stone. The people surrounding her thought there was a voice at the bottom of the garden, she stayed silent and kept it just hers not something she had to share.

She had shared so much of herself she was not willing to give them this.

She left and she found a place where she could wear the mask that was more comfortable. But no one was fooled by the façade. Even after they had broken through the toughened glass he used as protection even after she told the story.

There was just a refusal to stand with her. Anything else was easier, denial, disbelief, a declaration that they had lied.

Anything was easier than facing the fact of the dark place where stagnant water crept round her and unfurled her pain, till the sickness consumed and the fear turned to a numb feeling.

If you fought her if you challenged her, even sullied her, she understood. It was easier to just conform to the words than believe that anything could bring something different.

But then the Rennet came, the strange light feeling that something had moved forward. But she was already irrevocably broken and the more love tried to enter the more it was misunderstood.

But control was a language her mind spoke, to be manipulated and controlled beyond measure was something was so malleable she was like soft clay.

The more she crept into the corner the stronger he stood and eventually they all believed the narrative. It was happening again the same narrative like a politician who spoke the truth to the crowd and then forgot the promise. But they believed everything they were fed However she coloured the picture they changed the colour and didn't see the view from the same perspective.

Then the moon fell from the sky it brought destruction and pain like she had never felt. She begged to stay under the darkness but he no longer wanted to be her master. Then Manasseh broke what had been painted. He changed the colours not to compete but complement the view.

The distance began to open up to possibilities that she hadn't considered. She kept her escape route but she fled from the bushes and the fields where hope was lost and made a home where when needed the sea could carry her away.

Emma Canvas

Danger Zone
extract from 'Falling Away'

We only had about 10 or 15 minutes to get everything ready for opening the library. Everyone would go through their own routines, switching on lights, the public PCs, self-issue machines, opening blinds, taking the cash drawer out of the safe, logging on to the catalogue and checking emails etc. Part of my morning procedure always involved laying out an ever decreasing number of newspapers on the reading room table. On one occasion I was drawn to a headline about the former residents in the ghost city of Pripyat. Some 30 years on from the nuclear disaster at Chernoybl, the abandoned Ukrainian metropolis had been declared unsafe for 24,000 years.

'Heroes of the Soviet Union' - the honour bestowed upon evacuees and workers who returned to the devastating inferno to fight the fires. In 1986, the future was so bright you had to wear shades along with a blue worker's boiler suit and slippers. This was the same year that saw the Soviets launch the Mir Space Station, the disaster of the Space Shuttle Challenger and in dear ol' Blighty Fergie got hitched to Prince Andrew. On the Top Gun soundtrack, Kenny Loggins took us high into the 'Danger Zone'.

After opening the main doors, I went straight over to unload the trolley next to the self-issue. It was then I noticed someone had just returned a copy of Coupland's *Generation X*.

'Been a long time...' I said without thinking as I picked it up and quickly skimmed through my former companion until the pages fell open at the start of the *Monsters Exist* chapter. 'Radioactive!' I started to read the bit where Dag drops the jar of Trinitite from Alamogordo, 'where they had the first N-test...'

'Excuse me, do you work here?'

I looked up at a bronzed skin lady, her yellowy hair glittering in the sunlight.

'Yes, how can I help?'

'Where do I return this?'

She was holding a hardback of Harper Lee's second novel

'*Go Set a Watchman*'.

'Not a problem, I can do that for you on the self-issue'.

Within moments, I was back to Dag's episode with the bottle of plutonium in Claire's house. When the green glass beads explode and shoot *everywhere*. I picked up my old friend and sought refuge on one of the pods a little out of the glare of the opening rush.

'Possibly the most charmed object in my collection…'

Almost the same words Johnny used to describe his own bottle of radioactive dust. Before I moved to South East London, I rented a dishevelled flat with him and a South African couple on the fringes of the green belt. It was in a quaint little village above a set of shops directly opposite the Green Man. The pub was hardly a symbol of rebirth though. Trapped in our own minds the habits took hold while any other interests lost all importance. A modern melancholy poetic where eyes began to close and everything started to go through the motions. Johnny and I were embroiled in the infinite merry-go-round of writing, rehearsing, and recording and gigging having played in bands for years. His uncle was 'the poodle' bass player/lead singer from 80's new wave synth pop combo *Kajagoogoo*. With spiky hair and androgynous looks, their name came to be synonymous with a multitude of other one-hit wonders. Johnny played bass like his uncle, but nourished himself more on the kick of drugs and booze than filling the cap with infectious grooves. He thought of himself as a real ladies' man being half-Greek with dark curly hair, a slim build and large brown eyes, perfect for his much rehearsed 'little boy lost' look. 'Can I cane?' There was usually someone to sponge money and fags off before he moved onto the next unsuspecting victim.

Johnny was infatuated by the fictional character Tony Montana from Brian De Palma's 1983 film, *Scarface*. Part of the 125,000 *Marielitos* as the Cuban refugees came to be known, who landed in Florida with nothing. A mass exodus driven by the Cold War politics of a stagnant economy weakened under the grip of the U.S. trade embargo and Castro's irritation with detractors. After retiring himself as a dishwasher, Tony climbs the ranks of the criminal underworld to become one of the most powerful drug lords in Miami. It was probably the twisted rags to riches version of the American Dream that appealed most to Johnny. His fascination with the magnetism of the criminal world would become his undoing. He enjoyed referring to his old man as 'Shotgun Lou' after an unsavoury incident with a rowdy bunch of hooligans. The episode took place at the chip shop owned by his father near Wimbledon FC's old ground on Plough Lane. Johnny helped him out a couple of nights a week and usually headed onto a few clubs afterwards. It was during this period that he started to frequent the Blue Orchid night club in South East London. Formerly known as the Croydon Greyhound, that once hosted bands like *The Damned* and *The Buzzcocks*. The two-discotheque club was owned by Charlie Kray who ran it until 1997 just before he was jailed for a second time. A Met Police sting operation uncovered his involvement in smuggling millions of pounds worth of cocaine into Surrey and London. Johnny referred to him as 'his friend Charlie' and always maintained that he was charming and friendly. No one knew how he had got to know him, but Johnny always proudly displayed *'Villains We Have Known,'* a book penned by Charlie's infamous younger brother Reg. A product of the environment with his identical twin brother Ron (alias The Colonel), 'The Twins' ruled the East End with their gang 'The Firm' throughout the 1950s and 1960s. The paperback was signed by Charlie, and included a message dedicated to Johnny, 'The World is Yours…'

'Radioactive!' Johnny claimed to have received a jar of dust particles from Chernobyl off one of Charlie's hard-nosed geezers at the Blue Orchid. It festered somewhere in-amongst all the other piles of junk scattered around his bedroom. On the door he'd blu-tacked a crude mock-up of the '25 Cromwell Street' sign.

One Monday evening in winter time about 6pm, I arrived back to an empty flat. I'd been away for the weekend at the folks' place on the outskirts of Brighton. After opening the door, I quickly realised the entire place was shrouded in darkness. No one had fed the meter. Thankfully, a small play of light shone through the hallway and guided me to the kitchen at the far end. While I was feeling inside the drawers trying to locate a candle and some matches, a series of loud bangs on the front door interrupted my rummaging. It turned out to be a drugs raid, with four police officers responding to a tip-off from an unknown source at the Green Man. Even though it was murky, I could tell the two men were dressed in plain clothes while the women officers wore the traditional crisp uniform with high-vis vests. They thought I was bluffing about the electricity situation at first, but after testing a few switches one of them went racing downstairs and soon returned with a couple of torches. They turned my room inside out and found nothing. While they were having a quick debrief I stood in the shadowy hallway, staring up at Johnny's door. It made me nervous to think what kind of substances might be lurking in there. They split into pairs and began searching the remaining two bedrooms.

'I've got something here!'

One of them called out in a whiny, voice. He emerged like a spaceman from the gloom of Johnny's bear pit shaking a jar filled with something dark brown.

All five of us gathered in the hallway as he offered the find up to the search lights.

'What is it?'

'Looks quite smooth.'

'Taste it.'

'Could be a bad bundle?'

He shook the jar again and showed it to me.

'Come on, you must know what it is.'

Like a faraway memory slowly surfacing, I could hear Johnny's laughter lunging through the air, beating tentative wings along the walls.

'If I told you the truth, you would never believe me...'

Months later, Johnny was arrested for trying to pass counterfeit twenties at the local Esso garage. We'd all long moved out by the time he was sentenced. I heard he got something like 120 hours community service. Typically, instead of doing his penance he ended up disappearing to charm magic America. Chasing his dream in the land of opportunity with the tradition of finding any way possible to get what you want in life. Johnny the Greek we nicknamed him. No doubt I will never see him again...

David Banning

R.S. Thomas
- A Dislocation of Mind

In the name of the Father and of the Son and of the Holy Spirit –
Lord have mercy.
Amen.
In Pilgrim's Corner at the end of the world,
                                        God is absent, there is no word.

Aberdaron, the last staging post before crossing to Ynys Enlli. Three visits the equivalent of one to Rome. Suspended above the beach beneath a hallowed landscape, in fear, shadows rise and meet. The night announces its arrival from a dead sea with the wind weighty as a storm. Like a poisoned tooth of sin, nature sharpens the cold knife of discomfort.

Above the tidemark, split between the light, half-light and dark, a dislocated mind is possessed by the rising line of the grey Irish Sea. As the rollers break, a solitary figure in a cassock pulls on the rope of a single bell, the sally a little higher from balance to balance.

All the world's suffering in a quiet prayer space of the north nave, pews set in the round – Lord have mercy.

Beneath the icon of Christ ascending above Enlli, a flickering candle draws the eye to unholy chipped plaster. Missing in many places, it exposes the loud calm crackle of broken slats.

The troubles of the land overlooking the sea,
                    God is absent, there is no word.

A history in stone set against the northeast wall, carved in the late 5th or early 6th century in honour of two priests.

VERACIUS PBR HIC IACIT ('Veracius priest lies here')

SENACUS PRSB HIC IACIT CUM MULTITU DNEM FRATRUM PRESBYTER
('Senacus priest lies here with many brethren priest')

Old jokes, old myths
Blackened graffiti on dirty walls…

The body of Christ   silence…
The body of the church   in shadow…

No echoes – Lord have mercy.

In simultaneous modes of consciousness, an extension saved by music. From dark despair a melody rises against those that seek to ravage the land. Their business has taken possession of homes and put shackles on tongues. An offence to the ear, what have they done?
                    God is absent, there is no word.

Please be seated…

Let us pray…

Face-to-face with a recluse, his ramshackle white hair swept back and away from a face furrowed by severity.

A dweller in the long cave of darkness – ogre or serial obsessive?

The mind comes alive when a tall shadow glides along the curve of the bay. Guarding the arched gate of an old farmhouse, a Mini Clubman hides a view toward the Irish Sea. A tall thin body in faded blue shirt, grey trousers and a tie coloured Labour red, framed by an open porch.

In perfect English enunciation,
"There is no present in Wales,
and no future"

Turn the clock back…

After opening the big black book, the Lord wafts a cloud of dust into your face. In the struggle for breath, you cough loudly before gracelessly licking a finger. As the shadows watch each other, a prayer sits idly.

Outside space and time, a solitary nature mystic moves as he wishes.

They know this. They know that silence, slowness and bareness have always held appeal for you.

And minds of frightening vacancy are numbed by the harshness of labour…

NO SPEECH.

Have they any idea what you're doing? Their mute tongues and eyes fuddled with coldness asleep somewhere between earth and heaven.

Surrounded by order and design and assumptions of good character, you can see into the harshness of life.

In the brown bilge of earth hour by hour...

From the dark wood pulpit, you're with the Lord now...

"Men of the hills, and wantoners with your sweaty females" – today's orthodoxy is tomorrow's antiquity...

A pause...from the wooden truss echoes whisper over dry bones. The roof is listening and the after silence drops back down.
         God is absent, there is no word.

One evening, in the world of the body, pop music blares from a pub window...
'This will never do!'

Another pub, a question – 'Do you believe in God?'

Your smirk combined with raised eyebrow – 'That is not the right question. The question should in fact be – What sort of God do you believe in?'

Poetry is religion; religion is poetry…*a deus absconditus*
                                      God is absent, there is no word.

They forget how you spent entire nights with the dying. Lonely and obdurate under forbidding skies, driving the 100 miles round trip to Bangor and back. Over and over…Draped in the Cross with its arms out, pointing both ways on no through roads, despite shrugs of indifference.

Gloria.

A simple song in a language they might understand, spitting at their derisive bursts of laughter and narrow outlook.

Dach chi'n leicio yma?
Wrth fy modd.

'You like here?'
'In my element…'

Yes. In winter you walk wild and free in the fields, woods and hedgerows. Away from the mind-numbing nonsense that spews out of their big screens and long aerials.

Gloria.

In the half-light…your arrival at the Llŷn…at first, how they mocked your accent relentlessly. An exile among the scornful, skimming the deep of a dark whirlpool - *this lot*, wasting themselves in lands of mechanized affluence…Now the village is exposed, take the Saints' Road. It's nothing but a thoroughfare for ice cream vans and tourists. Who knows where the real Aberdaron is! Day in, day out, the awful industrial reverberations of English settlers…In between gales, the rush to snap up scattered houses. Like the repeated territorial disputes trumpeted by the choking calls of herring gulls. Sinking into sands at journey's end, the oval summit of Mynydd Mawr marks your cultural pilgrimage. Ringed by the setting sun, you lift those infant eyelids back some forty years to the beach at Holyhead. Forty miles westward, settling into the Wales of your dreams…

Gloria.

In the dark dynamism of confrontation, they suspected a traitor in their midst. English may be the language that opens doors, but who got the Post Office to put up the sign, *Y Llythyrdy*? From the green hills and sweet fields of Surrey, such enthusiasm painted by your English wife Elsi – an artist with large shadowy eyes. Other shops weren't so accommodating. The butcher laughed somewhat nervously at your suggestion of *Cigydd* ('High Class Butchers'). You could never understand the peculiarity of an upper-class sounding Englishman using only *proper* Welsh words.

Hello to the fresh hordes of tourists – NO ENGLISH

Without national consciousness – WHAT SONG

Sing a few outmoded hymns in winter – SHALL BE THEIRS?

Summer will bring the next influx of money, children and dogs – LEAVE IT, LEAVE IT

Cachau Bant why don't you. Tourism and low employment, despite all their pleasantries they easily outmanoeuvre that lot season by season. Like them you are trapped in your own misfortune. Born lost, the exiles within.

Gloria.

Dim Saesneg. Whenever any tourists stop to ask for directions you just throw your arms up in the air and shake your head at the same time. 'Oh, OK sorry to bother you Father!'

Gloria.

Reminders amongst a mass of contradictions…Reminders that some parishioners think you've more time for birdwatching than you have for them. Yes. In dreams, the mists of blue-wet horizons as you wait for the tides to recede. Gazing at the sea's foam the intoxicating sound of cormorants taking off from the coves of the peninsula fills the air. Sometimes as it goes on for weeks on end, you end up crunching pebbles on the beach over the swell of waves...

Looking honestly at the cruelty of the world

Violent

Imagination

Love bleeds on the untenanted cross...

God is absent, there is no word.

In the solitude of night, you kneel before the altar. By the melting candle's glimmer fingertips cling to a moment of calm, while the tide gnaws at the Bible. Seeking infinity, the vanquished envelop the sands and pursue you from the depths.

Where are You? Religion is over...

How long must you wait while your questions accumulate? Does the silence hint at disapproval or have you answered His deafness with your dumbness. This constant lack of acknowledgement has made you turn to a life in harmony with nature. Yes. Away from the ever-growing din of man's machines, without hope of a reply, art becomes necessity.

God is absent, there is no word.

In winter's robes you watched three sparrowhawks attempt to hunt down a green woodpecker. Those shrieks pierced right through your icy taut body, as it fled into a tree. But the three-winged gods followed in attack formation. You lodged a fist into your mouth and bit down hard into bone. In love's torment one soul to another sucking on skin gleaming red with fresh blood. Exiting the other side, you glimpsed the woodpecker, while the three of them ushered in a terrible beauty. Fastening their talons until a bloody rupture accelerated the end.

God is absent, there is no word.

Will they ever understand your long Welsh words? Take those imbeciles at the County Council putting up a new set of monoglot signs. Claiming it's due to an increase in the number of tourists. 'Whistling Sands' instead of *Porth Oer*...You tell them birds nesting on beaches suffer too. You tell everyone again and again - some species are leaving. And yet despite this constant anguish, now and then a rippled, but smoothed surface reflects the sun off the sea at different angles, lifting the misty gloom with illuminated paths of glitter. Yes. How sweet it was to see an oystercatcher's nest at the edge of Porth Wylan. You heard the loud cries struggling to protect three precious eggs nestled inside. Touched by their tenderness, you thought of picking up the nest within the palm of your hand to shield it from the encroaching chill of night.

Where are You? Religion is over.

A ghost in the dusk… *Tyto alba*. Heart-shaped face, buff back and wings with patches of pure white under parts. When first you came to the village you witnessed a barn owl nesting in the chimney of a cowshed. Once, the rare treat swooped down on the way home and paused on a wooden post a few yards ahead. In the perfect silence of twilight, you stood holding your breath admiring its wraithlike shape. Washed with golden feathers that barely whisper in the hush of flight, in grey parishes they swoop with intuition and mystery. You used to see merlins too, especially in winter. Catching larks and cars, those little lady falcons scanned their prey with freshly coloured slate-blue backs, rapid wingbeats, and square-cut tails…

Perhaps it is all a dream? Abandoning the deep shadow of His presence from the summit of Enlli, where the sadness rises in you like the sea.

God is absent, there is no word.

From the depths – you play over the final scene…

Dragged back into the waves, in cold shadows a mind cast, until a lobster pot is placed into the church…

Such wretched distress, a continual reminder whistles under the door.

Blown-in from the North-West for days without end…

Fallen from the seas a spiritual vortex filled with inner turmoil.

Those deep spaces of your anguished heart, a memorial left to a damned soul who could not be saved.

A body in the shadow of martyrs…

In silent communion, you could never ignore their grief like those who walked past you on the road.

Only the pain of speechless echoes - in or out of time – will He correct this?

No words or sounds...

Nothing except your endless search for nature in a Church you no longer believe in.

Alone...The last dance...

One less

and one less

and one less

You burn your cassock on the beach beneath the back door to the Vestry.

In the name of the Father and of the Son and of the Holy Spirit – Lord have mercy.

Amen.

David Banning

"The Real Eden Project"

Welcome to "The Real Eden Project" neural broadcast news. This week's real reality, and there's nothing virtual about it, is between these beeeautiful people. Mmm, tasssty. What a holy bash and a smash you're in for.

So join us, the temperature is hot, it's humid and we've got a real treat for you this week. A good old couple of stereotypes. Adam, the beefcake, thick as two short planks. Eve the sexy temptress, dangerous. And the serpent, he may be a wimp, but he's funny, charming and a real good listener. And very manipulative, to add to his endearing qualities.

But the real star of the show – the Tree of Knowledge with a real apple. Not many of these ultra-genetically modified beauties around, and we want to keep it that way. Supply and demand means you only get to taste the real fruit if you come on our show. They are simply Deee-vine.

Remember, each week we need an Adam, an Eve and a serpent. All you have to do is sign a waiver. We then temporarily wipe your memories and feed you mood enhancers. It's so exciting to see the natural interpersonal dynamics. And you get to keep the experience forever on all round Feel-o-Vision.

And what's more, it's your duty, like our elders told us at the freedom climate rebellion insurgency committee fundraiser tea dance… This show is all an experiment, we believe our broadcast is Goods and Services. And our Religion is Gods and Services.

And now, our omni-present narrator - the word of God!

[4] This is the story of the heavens and the earth when they were made, in the

day the Lord God made the earth and the heavens. ⁵ Now no bush of the field was yet on the earth. And no plant of the field had started to grow. For the Lord God had not sent rain upon the earth. And there was no man to work the ground. ⁶ But a fog came from the earth and watered the whole top of the ground. ⁷ Then the Lord God made man from the dust of the ground. And He breathed into his nose the breath of life. Man became a living being.

And here coming out of the mist is our new Adam !! Look at those muscles and the rest of it! So switch on your vision to explore the environment our bio-interior designers have created…

For those not joining us in our 3D environment, in haptic Feel-o-Vision. You don't know what you are missing. Remember you can experience the show from the eye sight of Adam, Eve, the serpent, or God, that's us of course. Replay from the different points of view. What an insight into life and art and religion. All in the name of "Science-Faction".

⁸ The Lord God planted a garden to the east in Eden. He put the man there whom He had made. ⁹ And the Lord God made to grow out of the ground every tree that is pleasing to the eyes and good for food. And He made the tree of life grow in the centre of the garden, and the tree of learning of good and bad.

Oh would you look at those trees, congratulations to the designers. Who've combined the unconscious ideals of our three contestants to produce these marvels for us all to delight in…

¹⁰ Now a river flowed out of Eden to water the garden. And from there it divided and became four rivers. ¹¹ The name of the first is Pishon. It flows around the whole land of Havilah, where there is gold. ¹² The gold of that land is good. Bdellium and onyx stone are there. ¹³ The name of the second river is Gihon. It flows around the whole land of Cush. ¹⁴ The name of the third river is Tigris. It flows east of Assyria. And the fourth river is the Euphrates. ¹⁵ Then the Lord God took the man and put him in the garden of Eden to work the ground and care for it. ¹⁶ The Lord God told the man, "You are free to eat *from any tree of the garden. ¹⁷ But do not eat from the tree of learning of good and bad. For the day you eat from it you will die for sure."*

So you hear that folks at home, the stakes are high. There is Eternal Life and death involved, and that is final. But don't worry, you can experience it time and again on "The Real Eden Project."

¹⁸ Then the Lord God said, "It is not good for man to be alone. I will make a helper that is right for him." ¹⁹ Out of the ground the Lord God made every animal of the field and every bird of the sky. He brought them to the man to find out what he would call them. And whatever the man called a living thing, that was its name. ²⁰ Adam gave names to all the cattle, and to the birds of the sky, and to every animal of the field.

So let's bring on all the fauna in the show. Ahhh, so cute to see the baby cows and sheep. Remember choose the red button to subscribe to the special option for life from their point of view.

But there was no helper found that was right for Adam. ²¹ So the Lord God put the man to sleep as if he were dead. And while he was sleeping, He took one of the bones from his side and closed up the place with flesh. ²² The Lord God made woman from the bone which He had taken from the man. And He brought her to the man.

And here she is, what a stunner, and remember you can now switch between Adam's view and Eve's whichever you prefer.

²³ The man said, "This is now bone of my bones, and flesh of my flesh. She will be called Woman, because she was taken out of Man." ²⁴ For this reason a man will leave his father and his mother, and will be joined to his wife. And they will become one flesh. ²⁵ The man and his wife were both without clothes and were not ashamed

And we certainly aren't ashamed here in the Eden studio or at home. But don't overthink the father and mother bit. Just assume God was both. But now, for the moment you've all been waiting for... Let's head to the Tree of Knowledge to meet the sssssss Serpenttt. Here he is, a skinny little weasel of a man with bio-attached tail and what a flicking forked tongue. Suits you sir. Sirrrpent that is.

$^{3.1}$Now the snake was more able to fool others than any animal of the field which the Lord God had made. He said to the woman, "Did God say that you should not eat from any tree in the garden?" ^{2}Then the woman said to the snake, "We may eat the fruit of the trees of the garden. ^{3}But from the tree which is in the center of the garden, God has said, 'Do not eat from it or touch it, or you will die.'"

^{4}The snake said to the woman, "No, you for sure will not die! ^{5}For God knows that when you eat from it, your eyes will be opened and you will be like God, knowing good and bad." ^{6}The woman saw that the tree was good for food, and pleasing to the eyes, and could fill the desire of making one wise. So she took of its fruit and ...
"Aarrghhh."

Here comes Adam bellowing out of the Jungle. The animals are running wild, scattering when they see him. His (ste)roid rage is palpable.

"You, you, dirty, cheating, princess!"

"I can't believe you just called me a princess. "

"She issss a princess, my princesss."

"And you, you slimy snake in the grass - God forbids you! Forbids You!!"

Ohh, look, Adam is grabbing his head, it looks like he's trying to twist it off. And the serpents face is going from green to blue to red. Now Adam's grabbed the apple off Eve...
"Now eat the flaming apple - you flaming, forbidden, snake!"

Ohh, Adam has shoved the apple into the mouth of our dear

departed Serpent. Ohh, he's turning to Eve, it doesn't look good. I think we better leave the show there but you can continue viewing if you switch to subscription adult only mode.

Well there we have it viewers, we never got to the end of the scenario, but what a ride. And despite all this fuss, no one today has actually eaten any of the apple. Even the Serpent didn't really take a bite. One day, if all three contestants are able to co-operate and make it through this whole section of Genesis, the Bible, then they will all be able to eat of that apple and will be made for life.

Right, so in the last show the Serpent and Adam became lovers. The show before that had them all go off to be alone. Next week a woman will be Adam, and man will be Eve, with a real shocker as to who the Serpent will be. So tune in to find out what amazing social dynamics are going to happen…

And we've had a message from one of our viewers. Mr Rodgers of Morecambe asks us whether by adding mood enhancer we are removing people's free will. Well Mr Rodgers, look at it this way, we are enhancing free will for your, our and their own entertainment. They are becoming more free to be who they really, really want to be.

And remember, playing God isn't what this is all about. Believing in God is the ticket. And you can get your free??? (a ha ha) ticket every week in "The Real Eden Project" neural network.

Anthony D Padgett

A Whole Sky

He hits snooze and rolls over. Morning spreads across the floor, through thin curtains, patterned blue and green swirls, ripples and dashes, like water, but no barrier against intrusion like the real thing.

He is swimming again, dropping his head underwater, pulling with his arms. Once fully immersed he drifts, feet paddling gently, using hands to steer this way and that. The water is clear, sounds of the world muffled. Bright vegetation sways with the current, golden, soft, lit by sunlight filtering through from above. Far off he hears the voice of a girl, singing a familiar song. He pulls his hands down, to propel himself forward, kicks hard with his feet, catching silt at the bottom. It clouds around him. He can't tell which direction she is, opens his mouth to call her, but it fills with water. Above him, maybe below, he hears a siren, its rhythm the same as the song. The water is dark, visibility restricted, his legs can't move, and his arms are rigid. The siren again, this time much louder.

Alarm goes off again, he hits snooze again, but it keeps on at him. He throws off the covers and swings his feet to the floor with a thud, sits a while, till his brain catches up with his body. Moves slowly through to the bathroom, across the landing. Feet thudding as he walks.

"Mum?"

No answer. Quick wash, quick spray, clothes on, he takes the stairs one two at a time. Last night's plates sit on the side in the kitchen, the fridge is pretty empty, milk smells rank. He swills the dishes to save her a job later, gazes out of the window to see a lifeless tea-towel hanging on the line – *Flowers of Britain* – none bloom in their garden. He dries his hands on his trousers, then back through to the hall.

"Mum?"

He climbs the stairs, pushes her door, just a crack, peers round to check how she is. She lies on her side of the bed, the other side empty, as if dad has just got out, or not yet come in. Dressing gown wrapped closely to her, frowning, even while sleeping, breathing deep and slow, covers pushed down, where they'd been the day before and she'd not made the bed. He pulls them back over her. The mirror reflects back the room, a boy tall-as-a-man, standing by her bed. Clothes litter the floor, where they've fallen or she's stepped out of them. He scoops them up, quickly, furtively, and throws them into the redundant laundry basket.

Downstairs, grabs his bag, checks the time, out the door and down the path. The sky is much lighter now, but it's a cold day, rain peeing down. Turns up the collar of his jacket against the wet. The walk is never pleasant, not much to look at. Paving slabs cracked, leaves drifted in heaps, he spots a dog squatting, so he doesn't kick through them. The uneven roads collect rain and passing cars spray dirty water up his legs. His bag hurts his bony shoulder, strap cutting in. The air is grey and the only noise is traffic crawling past, stopping and starting as cars reach the junction, pull out one by one. Tyres on wet tarmac, slurping and hissing. Houses with net curtains to keep the outside from peering in. Tiny lives in tiny rooms. A man comes out of number 34 and runs to the bus stop holding a newspaper above his head to keep off the rain. No point waiting for a bus, by the time one comes along you're soaked anyway. And the noise on them, tsk-tsk-tsk of secret music through headphones, chat-chat of girls, mindless banter from blokes in cheap suits.

He walks past the queue, silent until they step on board, as if the sanctuary of the vehicle loosens their tongues. Roddy Becks is there.

"Alright."
They exchange the word, with a toss of the head. He'll beat Becksy to the gates, he always does. He heads for Happy Shopper to buy a carton of milk. He loves milk, ice cold, to throw down his gullet as he walks along. Round the corner, through the door.

"Alright," from the girl behind the counter. He throws up his head in reply, chucking money on the side. Downs the milk, starts running to make up time. Through the gate, bell going. Along the hall, grey like the sky, climbs the puke stairs with matching puke walls, to French with 'Miller the Perve'. Granger's on duty along the top corridor, handing out flyers for some weirdo club he runs after school. Lessons drag on. He's got no lunch so blags some off one of the girls. They all like him, think he's dead sensitive, not bad looking. But he's no time for girls, knows what they're like under that sparkle, full of dreams that are bound to turn sour.

    Not a bad day, not too much aggro, he's pushed through the gate at the edge of the crowd. Turns up the lane, collar up, head down, for the walk home.

    "Getting the bus?" Becks shouts over.

    "Nah, I'll walk." Like he always does.

He'll run it, the back way. Takes longer, but the rain's stopped, bit of sun getting through, naked trees reaching to touch it, in case it can spark some leaves off to dress them up again. Long strides, breathing deep, even. Holding his bag close to stop it banging around. On up the hill, slipping on gravel and dirt, he runs, he trips, lunges, grabs to stop his fall, but falls anyway. And where his hand goes out to break the fall, he feels something, curved and hard. He grips it in his fingers, pulls his hand back to take a look. A shoe, resting in the palm of his hand. Miniature and neat, a Cinderella slipper, silver, with jewels that catch the weak rays of the sun and bounce them back, bright. He casts a glance around, nobody looking, so he puts it in his bag between geography and sports science, first picking off the bits of damp leaf that stick to it.

    Head down, walking now, not running, back towards the shops. Turns the corner and heads for home. Key in the door, slams it behind him, hears the voice from the front room.

    "That you?"

Who else would it be? He opens the door to find her as usual, in the chair, in front of the telly.

    "Alright," he grunts.

    "Alright love. Want some tea?" Said without looking up.

She never makes tea, just sits smoking, watching quizzes on telly. He puts his hand in his bag, curls his fingers round the shoe. And turning back to look at her, the light from the screen catches her hair, it glows gold and her face looks softer. The audience gasp and applaud on the telly.

    "Mum…" but it's already passed. He lets go of the shoe and

climbs the stairs. She sucks on the cigarette, lips smacking as she pulls it away, filter toffee brown where she drags so hard. The ashtray is full, balanced on the arm of the chair. Some man has just lost £16,000 because his final answer is wrong.

"Ahh," says Mum.

He runs a bath, drops his clothes on the floor and climbs in. Under water the sounds are muffled, steady beat of music from next door, dull sound of telly from below, a siren. It is warm in the water and as it cools down, he stretches up his foot and twiddles the tap to let in more hot until it slowly splurges out of the over flow and he has to get out because there's no more hot to put in. The immersion tank speaks to him, grumbling and complaining, as he throws on a t-shirt and steps into his jeans. He lifts her laundry basket under one arm, like a child balanced on his hip, takes it downstairs.

Not much in the freezer, couple of pizzas. He takes one out and slams it in the oven, watches her, watching telly, while it cooks through. He puts some on a plate, on the chair by her elbow. He knows she won't touch it, eats like a bird now, taste buds all gone. He lies on his bed gazing up at the ceiling, at the clouds she painted there when he was a kid. One looked like a witch and he'd cried, afraid it would get him. So she climbed on his bed, paintbrush in hand and daubed more white to paint it out, sung to him softly - *raindrops keep falling on my head* - until he drifted off to dream about being big and fighting all the monsters in the world.

Traffic outside, dog barking, music next door, telly mumbling down below. He drifts into sleep, doesn't hear her switch off the telly, climb the stairs, slowly, sigh at her reflection in the mirror, or the creak of the bed as she lowers herself onto her side of it.

In the morning, he forgets the shoe shoved inside his bag. He goes through the motions, same as every other day. Alarm, snooze, alarm, quick wash, quick spray, gets dressed, looks in on his mum. He walks the usual way, bag on his shoulder, banging in time with his stride. He feels a pain in his leg where something digs in. He slips his hand inside his bag and wraps his fingers around the heel of the shoe, feels along to the toe. The sun trickles weakly but the trees seem triumphant, the pavement shiny, the heaps of leaves like fires, he kicks his way through them, revelling in the swish. The sound fills his head.

"Oi, Becksy! Why don't you walk?" He shouts at the slumped figure of the boy as he passes.

"Nah. Too far," comes the reply.

"Alright mate," to the man at number 34.

"Who are you callin' mate?"

On to the shop, Happy Shopper – he *is* a happy shopper, round the corner, through the door, into the shop, carton of milk.

"Good morning," smiling to the girl behind the counter.

"Are you takin' the piss?" She glares at him.

He slugs down the milk, white, cold, spilling a bit on his jacket. Through the gate, he beats the bell, beats Becksy and starts the school day. The hall isn't grey, it's a soft kind of lilac, like that shirt mum wore when she worked at the bank. The stairs aren't puke, and Miller's just friendly, not like the old teacher who shouted and yelled. Granger's not weird, just into weird stuff, and that's okay.

He gets into trouble, asks too many questions, they're not used to him like this.

"What's your game?"

"You being funny boy?"

But not a bad day as days go, a bit too much aggro, but nothing he can't handle. He is pushed through the gate at the edge of the crowd and turns up the lane, collar up, head down, for the usual walk home. Past the arcade of shops, Pizza Panic, Booze Busters, Happy Shopper. He looks up at the hill behind, a whole sky up there. He takes a run at it, long strides, holding bag, hand on the shoe inside, breathing deeply and reaches the top. Spinning around he cries aloud like Tarzan. The sky is huge, the town is tiny, the grass is soft and dewy and the air is clear. He can see his whole life down there, and he is alive.

He runs home as fast as he can, shoe in his hand, tripping and stumbling, but not falling. Up the path, fumbling with his key, he barges into the front room, calling as he does.

"Mum! Come out for a bit. Mum?"

Mum with her golden hair that she has never dyed, that used to shine when he was a little kid, who used to laugh before dad had gone, who used to sing and dance, who used to paint and draw mad pictures with him and cook and bake whilst he made potions and special recipes by her side, who sits in a chair mostly now, cigarette in hand, motionless, shineless, songless.

He hears the immersion tank grumbling and complaining, gurgling and refilling up in the bathroom and takes the stairs three at a time. She lies in the bath, hair streaming like Ophelia, not golden now, but dull. An empty strip of pills lying on the floor. He uncurls his fingers from the muddy old shoe and lets it drop to the floor. He kneels beside the bath and wonders if he should lift her out before she gets cold and wrinkled but instead leans forward and turns on the tap to let in a little more hot.

Anne Holloway

Of Course
It Was The Sky That Drew Me Here

On some days you can see the curve of the planet.
The light changes in a breath.
Look at that I say with a sweep of my arm.
    We could be on Lake Garda.
When the rain comes, it swathes the hills in soft greys.
I have lost count of the number of photographs I have taken.
That sky. In the foreground the curve of the pale blue bollards.
And when the rain has gone, the sand flats glisten.
Silvered mirrors, reflecting the sky.

Anne Holloway